QI LAI!

MOBILIZING ONE BILLION CHINESE:
The Chinese Communication System

DATE DUE

QI LAI!

MOBILIZING ONE BILLION CHINESE: THE CHINESE COMMUNICATION SYSTEM

Robert L. Bishop

 IOWA STATE UNIVERSITY PRESS / AMES

**This book is fondly dedicated
to my best teacher,
HO MAN WAH**

ROBERT L. BISHOP is Professor of Journalism and Mass Communication, Henry
W. Grady School of Journalism and Mass Communication, University of Georgia,
Athens. He was Aw Boon Haw Visiting Lecturer in Mass Communications,
Chinese University of Hong Kong, 1980–81.

© 1989 Iowa State University Press, Ames, Iowa 50010
All rights reserved

Composed by Iowa State University Press from author-provided disks
Printed in the United States of America

First edition, 1989
International Standard Book Number: 0–8138–0296–2

. **Library of Congress Cataloging-in-Publication Data**
Bishop, Robert L., 1931–
    Qi lai!

    Bibliography: p.
    Includes index.
    1. Mass media—China.   I. Title.
P92.C5B57   1989   001.51′0951   87–36153
ISBN 0–8138–0293–8
    0–8138–0296–2 (paperback)

CONTENTS

PREFACE

This book has taken shape over several years as I became more and more engrossed in the study of China. I have come to admire the Chinese people and to realize the immensity of Western ignorance about all things Chinese. Therefore this book is offered as an introduction to the Chinese communication system with some trepidation. It is my hope that it will open a few doors by showing that many of the same factors that shape Western ways of communicating are at work in China. At the same time, I do not wish to make too much of supposed similarities; China is China and not to be trivialized by over facile explanations.

The title of the book is taken from the Chinese national anthem, "Qi Lai!"—"Stand Up!" It epitomizes the aim of the People's Republic and also points out the tremendous task that challenges their best—the mobilization of one billion people with the help of the Chinese communication system.

Qi Lai!

Stand up, all you who refuse to be slaves!
With our blood and flesh a great wall will be built.
The Chinese nation now faces its greatest danger.
From each comes forth his loudest call:
Stand up! Stand up! Stand up!
Millions as one, braving the enemy's fire, march on.
Braving the enemy's fire, march; march on, march on and on!

A word about transliteration. The People's Republic has abandoned the old Wade-Giles method for a new system called pinyin, which means "phonetic spelling." Suddenly Canton became Guangzhou, Mao Tse-tung turned into Mao Zedong, and so forth. I have used the old system for historical references and for those Chinese who did not adopt the new system but followed modern practice for everything since 1949, the year that the People's Republic came into existence. In that way, anyone wishing further information will be most likely to find the name listed in current reference sources in the same way I have used it. For the inevitable mistakes, I beg forebearance.

Many people have contributed to my understanding of China. To them, my thanks and wish that I could have been a better student. I would especially like to thank Mrs. Chung Yau Ling, whose thesis started this whole long journey. My students and colleagues at the Chinese University of Hong Kong contributed greatly, especially with the studies of *The Southern Daily* and *The People's Daily.*

I would also like to thank Professor Everett Rogers of the Annenberg School of Communications, University of Southern California, and Professor Leonard Chu of the Department of Journalism, Chinese University of Hong Kong, for their helpful suggestions after reading an early draft.

QI LAI! MOBILIZING ONE BILLION CHINESE:
The Chinese Communication System

1 FROM FEUDALISM TO PEOPLE'S CAPITALISM— A PERSONAL VIEW

From past to present

ESTEEMED ELDER BROTHER,

Many years have passed since you left our village for Hong Kong. We are happy to hear that you have prospered, and thank you for the television set you sent. While there have been many changes in our little village of Wu zhao, we are well and happy to be together.

You ask about changes in our family life since China's liberation in 1949. One can almost agree with the cadres (the Party workers) that the Party has become our family, but the situation is not so simple as that.

As you know, we have lived through much turmoil. When the Communist party workers arrived in 1949, they began by finding everyone who had grievances against landlords, money-lenders, or political leaders. When they identified some poor peasants, they held long discussions to prove that their individual problems were part of a class struggle.

I have chosen this fictional example of change in a Chinese village to begin this volume because it allows me to express the personal side of the forces and trends that have swept China throughout its history. At the center, however, is the individual, with whom all communication originates. The letter is based on actual cases and on our own interviews with 236 Hong Kong immigrants in 1981. The letter represents conditions in Guangzhou (Canton) around 1980, and in much of the rest of China as late as 1985. The Guangzhou area was one of the first to go to the "responsibility" system under which a great deal of capitalistic techniques, mentioned here by the younger brother, were reintroduced.

Once some poor peasants could be persuaded to publicly accuse people who had offended them, the cadres had mass meetings for all the poor and middle-class peasants. They spit on the rich peasants and landlords as class enemies and whipped up the crowd until everyone joined in. In some places, the "bad classes" were immediately tried, humiliated, beaten, jailed, or even killed. Our rich families had already escaped to Hong Kong, so only a few people were jailed. Property was redistributed, giving poor peasants a reason to join the liberation movement.

To be sure that we all learned what was required of us, the cadres held mass meetings for the entire village, discussion groups for women and young people, parades, and demonstrations. They wrote *tatzebao* — big character posters — and posted them on the walls of the village. They took over the school and made all the children learn Chairman Mao's sayings. Since most of us could not read or write (including the cadres), the few cadres who were literate read the Party newspapers to us.

Land reform, communes, and the whole new system of government were in the hands of cadres from places far away from our little village. They didn't even speak our dialect! We did not know or trust them, and they did not know local conditions. Some bad characters filled their own pockets. Some were just bureaucrats who sat in their offices and filed false reports with Beijing. Some were farmers but did not know how to run an entire commune.

At first, several villages were put together in one production brigade. That proved too difficult — too many disagreements between villages with good land and villages with poor land, between families, and between clans. Also, the cadres were not experienced enough to manage such a large enterprise.

Worse than the commune movement was the Great Leap Forward. That was the time in 1958 when Chairman Mao told us to modernize the country overnight. But plans for revolutionizing the farms and factories were a complete failure, and we went through some hungry years before getting back on our feet. Then we were hit by the Cultural Revolution, beginning in 1965, when the chairman urged young people to form Red Guard brigades to get rid of anyone who was even suspected of opposing the leftist radicals.

We handled that situation by forming our own young people into a Red Guard battalion. When outsiders came in and tried to tear down everything we had built up since Liberation, our own Red Guard defended us. And then, of course, the People's Liberation Army from Guangzhou finally took command.

But now things have settled down and we can hope once more. The work unit has been reduced to the village again, and our own kinsmen are the team leaders. They are more trusted, and they know more about local conditions. So a feeling of family connections is important once more. Families are allowed their own plots of land, in addition to working for the commune, and the commune can keep everything that it produces beyond the taxes that the government collects. We think that production has risen because of the new conditions — our own leaders can be depended on to be fair in assigning work points, arranging credits, and so on — and I know we are much happier.

Many things have changed, especially for women and young people. You remember, I am sure, how our esteemed father was an absolute ruler. All property belonged to him and all decisions were made by him. He even chose our wives — I don't think you had ever seen Elder Sister-in-law until your wedding day!

The women of the house, especially young wives who had not yet had children, were ruled by our mother, and she could be a tyrant! It was a blessing from heaven to be born male! Women had no right to property or even to their own children. They could not get a divorce or even complain of beatings and ill treatment. I'm sure you remember Wong hua, who beat his wife to death because she did not produce a male heir. Since her family was weak and could not defend her, no one reproached Wong hua.

Now women are supposed to be completely equal. Sometimes they are still mistreated by their husbands, but if they wish, they can go to court and get a divorce. They own property and have equal rights of inheritance. They take leading roles in the Party and get work points (our system for deciding how much of a share of the farm or factory income each person gets) equal to men for working in the fields or factories, as most of them do. (Few families could live if both the husband and wife did not work full time. Everyone must work to build up the new China.)

Liu Man Wah, for instance, was left a widow with two children to support. She met a man from the Deng family and wished to remarry. But her in-laws refused, saying that they had bought her and that she was obligated to support them. They also claimed the male child, though they did not care what happened to the girl. Liu Man Wah took them to court, and the court decided that she was free to remarry and to take her children and was entitled to her husband's share of the family inheritance.

In the old days, the government had nothing to do with our little village except to send the tax collector around. The family clan took care of law and order. The Council of Elders was our court. It settled disputes, mediated with other clans, arranged for the veneration of ancestors, paid for the village school, and took care of clan members who were destitute. We had our own small militia and, even though we were only seven miles from Guangzhou, we had little help from or use for government.

Now all that has changed. Since Liberation, the Party controls everything, and we elders have been put aside. Oh, we still have our Five Guarantees — the Party will see that we have food, clothes, shelter, medical attention, and a burial if we have no children to provide for us. But since all property belongs to the state now, we have no economic power. Young people count today. Old folks are considered too set in their ways, too illiterate, too capitalist-tainted.

Instead of working with their elders on the family farm, young people are assigned jobs by the commune. It is the commune and the Party that decide whether they go to school or not, and even some poor peasant families now see their children in technical schools and universities.

Many youngsters do not revere their elders at all, although the Party teaches that you must take care of your parents. During the early days, it is true, some children informed on their parents as counterrevolutionaries, just because of something they may have said in anger. And during the Cultural Revolution, young people were encouraged to show all manner of disrespect. Many good people were even killed, although I do not think that many of the young revolutionaries attacked their own families if they could avoid it.

Half the young men in our village have left to find work elsewhere, some in the People's Liberation Army, some with factories and government work in the city, and many in Hong Kong. But most send money back to help their relatives, just as in the old days.

Another area that has changed greatly is communication between our little family village and the rest of the world. Before Liberation, we had no newspaper, radio, or television. Some rich families lived in Guangzhou most of the time, and of course they could get newspapers and listen to the radio there. We picked up some news when we went into the city to sell produce and swapped information in the teahouses and at the market in the next village. But the rest of the world had little to do with us and we knew little about it.

That changed as soon as the first cadres arrived in 1949. One of their jobs was to break down our provincialism and to make us see that we are part of all China.

During the Great Leap Forward, wired radio loudspeakers were brought into the village. It worked like this. Most programs came from Beijing. Each county seat had a wireless receiver that could rebroadcast the programs, adding some programs of its own. Then wires like telephone wires were strung to each village and loudspeakers were placed on poles so that every house could hear the broadcasts. Since our little village has only about 100 homes, this was not hard.

For a while, the Party published a newspaper in the county seat, but it cost too much to run and too few people could read it. So the newspaper was shut down, but the wired radio stays.

Now we have movie teams who travel from village to village with films about killing insects, birth control, better farming techniques, and so on. Sometimes they even bring entertaining films! Also, the Party or the army sends actors to put on revolutionary plays.

In recent years families have been able to afford their own newspapers, magazines, radio, and even television. Since we live near Hong Kong, it is possible to receive radio and television programs from there. During the Cultural Revolution, of course, this was very dangerous. But no one seems to mind now.

We have two newspapers from Guangzhou, *The Southern Daily* and *The Ram City News*. In addition, there is *The People's Daily, The Liberation Army Daily,* and publications for young people, peasants, students, and many other groups. We can either buy a subscription or read them in the commune library.

The cadres have special meetings and newspapers that are not available to us, but they tell us whatever we need to know. And of course, there is always the "Little Road" news—the grapevine. Most of us have some family member who lives in Beijing or have some connection with a talkative official!

Sometimes it is difficult to know what to believe. Of course, it is necessary to follow the official newspapers and group meetings in order to know what the government is saying. We can depend on them for routine information. But we try to verify any important news with someone we know personally.

For example, many of our relatives have gone to Hong Kong, in spite of all the warnings from the Party. Some of them are quite naive about life there, I am sure. But they compared official information with what they got in letters from Hong Kong and what they saw when relatives came to visit and decided to trust their relatives more than impersonal sources.

I don't mean to say that everything is easy. We understand that it will take a long time to build a strong socialist state that need not fear its neighbors. Farm life in China has always been hard, and it is not easy now. Poor peasants are better off than they were, but middle-class peasants who used to own two or three acres of land get less from their share of the commune's production than they did from their own farm. We do not have beggars or prostitutes—at least not many—or children sold into slavery or abandoned to die, or people starving to death.

It is true that the responsibility system has brought some spiritual pollution. Materialism has replaced patriotism, at least in many homes in this district. People are convinced that "to get rich is glorious," and they have even made schools and medical centers into profitable instead of socialist enterprises. We have some scandalous tabloid newspapers that just carry stories of sex, scandal, and the supernatural. Some young men have opened theaters where you can pay to see videotaped programs and movies from Hong Kong. I have heard that some of these are very pornographic.

We hope that you can return for the Ching Ming festival. Although our ancestral hall is now Party headquarters, we are allowed to "sweep the graves of our ancestors" privately.

With deep respect, I remain

YOUNGER BROTHER

An overview of change

I have chosen to focus on the 80 percent of Chinese who live in the 1 million villages rather than on the urban dweller. Certainly, the cities cannot be ignored in a communications study, since most media originate near urban centers of commerce and power. But the villages have spawned peasant revolts throughout history and riots and demonstrations even today. The greatest challenges to communication and national development are in the countryside. It is the essential conservatism of the Chinese farmer that the Communist party must deal with if it is to modernize the Chinese nation. And it is with the traditional kinship system (always the only guarantee of security for peasants) that the national political and economic system must work.

As I have pointed out (Bishop 1983), the close-knit family group forms a closed, face-to-face, wheel-like system of communication, strongly resistant to outside influences. (The comparison to a wheel comes from the fact that while one person may be dominant, just as the spokes of a wheel are all connected to the hub, every person on the rim of the wheel is connected to everyone else in the group.)

The Communist cadres attempted to change this traditional system to a hierarchical pattern, responsive to orders and direction from the top down, so as to mobilize society. The hierarchical system is well suited to emergency mobilization — to armies moving at the direction of a single person. But it is weak because it does not involve the individual except as he or she follows orders. In the long run, it does not enlist loyalty or a sense of belonging and hinders individual initiative. Once the emergency is gone, the hierarchy rules only by force.

Since the downfall of the Gang of Four (Chairman Mao's wife and her cohorts, who tried to seize absolute control after Mao's death in 1976), there have been repeated, though uncertain, attempts to modify the hierarchical pattern to enlist fuller participation. The Party has tried to decentralize authority and responsibility and, along with them, communications. This more closely resembles what I call a star pattern. Each commune or factory has face-to-face communication or "wheels," but the wheels are linked to a central point. The commune is linked to the county, county to province, and province to the nation's capital, in a star configuration.

Another important feature of a mobilizing society is cross-group membership. The Chinese now belong to a number of groups cutting across traditional lines. Young people may enlist in the Young Pioneers (a version of the Party for elementary school children) and later in the army. Women belong to national organizations for women. Ex–Red Guards have a network of acquaintances across the country. The Cultural Revolution at least worked to break down some of the exclusiveness and provincialism of the peasant, since young people were encouraged to travel around the country at government expense, either to attend rallies or to reenact the Long March—the epic retreat by the Communists to the northwestern part of China in the 1930s.

THE FAMILY

A traditional Chinese point of view is well expressed by Liang Shu-ming, (quoted in Yang 1965, 166–67),

The widower, the widow, the orphan, the aged without children—these suffer the greatest misfortunes of a normal life, and they are (traditionally) called the "inarticulates." They are so called because they have no loved ones to whom they can tell their stories of sickness, hardship, poverty, and misfortune. . . . For the Chinese, the family is the fountainhead of his life and the place which he regards as his final repose. It is extremely difficult to stabilize life except by the tie of the family. Life usually brings more grief than joy, but the family provides the sentiments of joy. To the Chinese people, the family provides consolation and encouragement, and practically performs the function of religion.

Not even the Cultural Revolution could break up the family. Several instances in which children were forced to go through the motions of denouncing their parents are related in Liang and Shapiro (1983) but this took place only under extreme circumstances and principally in the cities. Family cohesion is related to the Chinese respect for authority. One's elders were authoritative, whether their deeds merited such respect or not. This deeply engrained tradition has not been easily changed.

Parish and Whyte's (1978) analysis of the Red Guard movement makes several important points. First, not all authority was challenged — only "unworthy" officials. Second, most students, factory workers, and peasants were very reluctant to attack local authorities. Many joined "conservative" factions, some sponsored by the officials under attack. Third, the family as such was not denounced.

Mosher's (1983) peasants could not believe that any child would be so unfilial as to turn on his parents. Only one man in the village that Mosher studied had denounced his father, a former landlord. The denunciation helped the son become a minor official in the commune, but he was regarded as beneath contempt. This was in spite of the fact that his father had abandoned the family and fled to Hong Kong, starting a second marriage there, before the denunciation. The peasants often denounced the father themselves but, though it had been thirty years since the son had foresworn his father, the incident had not been forgotten. Nor does the migration of young people necessarily weaken the family.

True, the Chinese kinship pattern began to change long before 1949. Modernization, education, urbanization, war-enforced mobility, and political pressures were breaking down the particularism of familial loyalty, making the peasantry psychologically available for broader loyalties.

But the family today is still primary. Chinese studies show that, while the linear family unit is declining, several factors work to maintain large families. First, both Chinese tradition and the new socialist moral code stress the responsibilities of parents for children and children for parents. Second, the two generations may be economically dependent upon each other. (Many young people depend on their families for housing and for the $1,500 or so necessary to set up housekeeping. Parents in turn still rely upon their sons for support in old age. In rural China, both generations work together as an economic unit. Even factory and government jobs and the right to live in the city are inherited.) Third, the elderly often want at least one child to remain with them. Fourth, a housing shortage forces some doubling up.

The old system of arranged marriages bound the family together as an economic unit. Arranging the marriage without asking either the bride or groom reinforced the idea that the new couple's allegiance was to the husband's family, not primarily to each other. The parents reaffirmed their dominance over the son and asserted their control over the wife.

Naturally, the new regime has tried to abolish arranged marriages, especially the practice of a bride price, which theoretically reimbursed the bride's family for the loss of her future labor. The campaign to enforce the new marriage law is outlined in Yang (1965, 7, 8). But he reports continued instances of arranged marriages. The heavy propaganda campaign was called "a light breeze that leaves no traces at all."

GOVERNMENT

Pre-Communist formal government stopped at the county level. Below that, clans and villages were held collectively responsible for taxes, defense, and administration. The commune movement was an attempt to reshape loyalties, authority, and communication. After its collapse, local government was largely returned to the clans, although the Party maintained a much greater presence than its predecessors. Parish and Whyte (1978) found that three-fourths of all small villages and neighborhoods within large villages (which make up production teams) consist of a single clan. Their informants reported that their 446 neighbors included 2 percent landlords, 4 percent rich peasants, 3 percent upper-middle peasants, 13 percent middle peasants, 4 percent lower-middle peasants, 73 percent poor peasants, and 2 percent dependent on overseas Chinese.

Sons and even grandsons of "bad classes" continued to have

difficulty until the mid-1980s. They were docked one work point a day, cutting their income by 10 percent. Barred from politics and desirable factory jobs, they had difficulty finding brides.

Butterfield (1982) makes the point that the government had to accept production teams based on small villages, clans, or neighborhoods in the larger villages as the basic agricultural production unit. This made collective farming acceptable and reinforced the peasant's interest in productivity. But it also gave the peasant more influence over the cadres, who tended to be relatives or neighbors.

ECONOMIC CONDITIONS

An illustration of a comfortable standard of living in Hunan in 1955 was given in a Chinese Communist report. The Li household spent about $92 on their six family members in a year's time. This bought 1,737 pounds of husked rice; 600 pounds of melon; 18 pounds of cooking oil; 45 pounds of salt; and small amounts of bean curd, salted beans, sugar, soybeans, vermicelli, and gourmet powder, plus 72 Chinese feet of cloth, 6 pairs of stockings, 1 pair of rubber shoes, about $4 for the expenses of their private farming, and $4 for medical expenses.

When Liang and Shapiro (1986, 60–62) revisited the village to which Liang had been exiled during the Cultural Revolution, they found that the villagers in 1985 were much better off. Still, the village had no electricity, many rooms smelled of "blackness and poverty," and there was irony in the villagers' boast, "Now even girls can eat rice!" This is in sharp contrast to villages near Hong Kong, where "10,000 yuan farmers" are touted as the equivalent of capitalist millionaires (10,000 yuan is roughly the equivalent of $6,000 per year).

In 1973, Guangzhou workers made 55 yuan per month (about $40 at that time), plus fringe benefits such as free medical care and a pension. Rural labor got only about half as much, including cash and produce from both the cooperative and a private garden or enterprise. Medical care was only partially subsidized, and there seemed to be no pension system. The peasant's salary was not paid until the harvest and depended on the crop.

By 1983, cash income per family averaged 600 yuan, and

corn yields per acre were 150 percent of 1979 yields in Dazhai, a village famous for its fictional exploits in the agricultural application of Mao's thought (Liang and Shapiro 1986, 219).

Nationally, rural income per person was reported at about $122 per year in 1983, while urban salaries were $207 (Scherer 1985, 90). The discrepancy in favor of city life continues, even though economic growth has been faster in the countryside.

SOURCES

Two works of particular usefulness in examining rural life are Yang (1965) and Parish and Whyte (1978). More recent and certainly more controversial is Mosher's (1983) story of his stay in China. Chan et al. (1984) give an invaluable picture of a village near Hong Kong. Madsen (1984) deals with the same village. Schell (1984) gives a useful view of the drawbacks to the new responsibility system as well as a sympathetic look at China in the 1980s. Liang and Shapiro (1983, 1984, 1986) have written unique reports on the Cultural Revolution and its aftermath, especially as it affected intellectuals.

2 PERSUASION AND THE FAMILY IN THE PEOPLE'S REPUBLIC

How effective are the Communist communication systems? Does anyone read the newspapers, listen to the wired radio broadcasts, sit through the small-group meetings, or cheer for the political campaigns now that the Gang of Four is gone? We turned to the Chinese themselves to find out. Hong Kong is full of recent illegal immigrants from the People's Republic, and we held extensive interviews with 236 who arrived between 1978 and 1981. Most, we found, came to Hong Kong to get a better job, often with the encouragement of their families, who depend on the money they send home.

Getting to Hong Kong is no easy matter. Sometimes the People's Republic is very tough on would-be emigrants, throwing them into county jails or heaping fines on them and/or their families. At other times, the Communists do not seem to care, but the alarmed British sweep back the tide of refugees. Yet they still come, sneaking across the border on foot, swimming Mirs Bay with its sharks and currents, hiding in boxcars, or paying

This chapter is based on Chung Yau Ling's master's thesis at the Chinese University of Hong Kong, where Dr. Bishop was Aw Boon Haw Visiting Lecturer in Mass Communications. We gratefully acknowledge the assistance of Professor Timothy Yu and Dr. Jiann Hsieh of the CUHK faculty, invaluable members of the graduate committee.

15

"snakeheads" to bring them across in high-speed motor launches. Many die in the attempt. They are not typical of the 1 billion Chinese who did not emigrate, but the fact that they were primarily looking for better jobs and that material published by the Chinese themselves indicates that similar attitudes exist among those who do not leave made us feel that the picture of the communication system they drew is reasonably accurate.

Methodology

There is no central point for reaching immigrants, so we used five different contacts: squatter communities where the newest immigrants live; their adult education centers; welfare organizations; the Wanderers Association, which fights for their recognition and rights in Hong Kong; and personal friends and relatives. The resulting sample was limited to people arriving after 1978. The Hong Kong government has surveyed the immigrants annually since 1970, although the survey was reported for the first time in the fall of 1980. During the last six months of 1979, 13,594 illegal immigrants were questioned as they registered for permanent papers—a 25 percent sample. Based on demographic data in these surveys, our sample appears to be representative as to age, social class, occupation, sex, and marital status.

Immigrants between 17 and 30 years of age made up 87 percent of the government sample. Less than 2 percent were over 41. Males accounted for 79 percent, and about 11 percent of them were married. Nine percent were from cities, 79 percent from villages, and 12 percent had been forcibly relocated from city to village. Some 43 percent had completed junior high; and 17 percent, high school. Less than 1 percent had completed technical or university courses. Ninety percent had relatives or friends in Hong Kong.

Our sample included 162 men and 74 women, of whom 108 were between 15 and 20 years of age; 88 were between 21 and 25, and 40 were 26 or older. Villagers numbered 106, while 60 were from small towns, and 70 were from big cities. Only 28 were married. Sixty-two had a primary school education or less,

76 had finished junior middle school, and 98 had gone to upper middle school, high school, or beyond. There were 20 professionals, 56 workers, 66 peasants, 92 students, and 2 handicraft workers. There were 62 with parents from the "black," or "bad," social classes: 36 professionals, 17 capitalists, and 9 landlords. Of the 164 from "red" families, 96 were peasants, 65 were workers, and 3 were military personnel.

Because we cannot say that our sample is random or representative, we have used nonparametric measures insofar as possible. However, a comparison of parametric and nonparametric measures gave few indications of serious distortion.

Our interviews were conducted in March and April 1981 by Chinese University graduates in sociology with at least two years of research and interviewing experience. They were guided by a questionnaire constructed and pretested by the author and Chung Yau Ling, a graduate student at the Chinese University who wrote her thesis on the study. The questionnaire covered four major topics: (1) background information, (2) family situations in China and Hong Kong, (3) media use and credibility in China, and (4) key factors affecting the decision to migrate. Some open-ended questions were included as well. Mrs. Chung also conducted thirty in-depth interviews, lasting from one to three hours, with selected respondents.

Findings

Some of our results will be presented in the form of interviews with three composite characters: Wen Jian Qing, Li Lin, and Aw Fang. None are real individuals; each represents a composite of what we heard from several different respondents.

Wen Jian Qing, a 30-year-old factory worker from Guangdong, is the oldest of the group. He left a wife and child, hoping to bring them to Hong Kong once his own status was legalized. (Until the fall of 1980, the Hong Kong policy was "touch base"—if you eluded the border guards and made it all the way to downtown Kowloon or Hong Kong, you had a right to stay. By 1981, however, illegals were deported whenever and wherever they were found.) By all measures, Wen was an unusual immigrant. Only about one in twelve of our immigrants is married. Two-thirds are male, and four out of five are less than 40 years of age. Almost half, in fact, are between 15 and 20. Only three out of ten are from big cities such as Guangdong.

Li Lin, a 21-year-old girl from a small village near Guangdong, had been sent down to the country during the Cultural Revolution. Originally a fervent Red Guard, she gradually burned out because of constant shifts in policy. "One day the earth is round, the next it is flat," she concluded after telling us of the reactions in her village to the supposed treachery of Liu Shao-qi, Lin Biao, and finally Jiang Qing herself. "We realized that it is not possible to believe all the preposterous things we were told, especially when they would all be turned on their heads at the next minute." Li Lin finished high school before being sent down, but most of her education consisted of political indoctrination. "Sure, we chanted the sayings of Chairman Mao," she admitted. "At first, we really believed everything. Later we realized that anything we said could be dangerous—so we stuck to slogans."

Aw Fang, a male peasant of 18, left the farm because every young person in his village had escaped. "It just seemed the normal thing for a young man to do," he said. "Until the family was allowed to keep what we made, above taxes, there was no hope for getting out of the mud. I could see I was doomed to be a peasant all my life. A peasant's life is very hard. Often we starve because some bureaucrat demands we grow crops that aren't suited to our climate, or build factories that have no raw materials and no market. On top of that, the laziest person in the village gets almost as much as the hardest worker. No, it seemed to me that life would be better in Hong Kong."

MOTIVES FOR EMIGRATING

Less than 3 percent of our sample fled China for political reasons (Table 2.1). Two-thirds migrated to improve living conditions for themselves and/or their families. Almost four out of five had been living in a two-generation family, mostly with their parents. In Hong Kong, however, two out of five lived in a single-generation household, and one in three lived with a cousin, uncle, or some more distant relative.

TABLE 2.1. **Motives for leaving China**

Reason	Percent
Political	2.8
Following other persons	14.6
Improving family standard of living	36.8
Improving personal standard of living	64.2

Note: N = 212; multiple responses allowed.

A study of the historical patterns of Chinese immigration (Chen 1940) indicates that economic pressures and family ties account for more than 88 percent of the cases. More than 40 percent of Chen's respondents moved because they were unemployed or underemployed and wanted to seek their fortunes overseas. Another 30 percent emigrated to improve the family's economic status. About 20 percent moved because of family or social ties with their new country.

Parish and Whyte (1978) point out that traditionally many young people have left Guangdong to go abroad. Two counties have half as many citizens living abroad as they have left in China. In the mid-1950s remittances from abroad to the county of Tai-shan were 120 percent of the annual farm income for the county.

MEDIA USAGE

Since much of what follows in this chapter is based on our respondents' access to information, it is reasonable to examine first their ties to the mass media. Wen and Li were avid media consumers in the People's Republic, with their own copies of both national and local newspapers. Wen even had access to his parents' television set, and Li and Aw could watch in their unit's lounge. Generally, media usage is high, ranging up to 73 percent for wired radio and films, compared to 46 percent for newspapers (Table 2.2). Nine out of every ten professionals and workers like Wen read newspapers, and seven of ten students; but only four of ten peasants like Aw do so. Eight of ten professionals watched television regularly, followed by six of ten workers and half the students. Professionals, being more literate, do the most reading. Probably the low figure for wired radio in their case indicates their greater access to radio and television and the

TABLE 2.2. Media usage in the People's Republic of China (percentage reporting regular use)

Medium	Entire Sample	Professionals	Workers	Peasants	Students
Wired radio	72.9%	60%	78.6%	75.7%	69.5%
Film	72.9	50	82.3	75.8	71.1
Newspapers	46.0	90	89.0	42.0	70.0
Radio	65.3	80	85.2	60.6	54.4
Television	47.5	80	57.2	31.2	48.9

fact that professionals are more likely to live in cities where wired radio is less compulsory. Fewer peasants read newspapers, because of illiteracy and distribution problems, and are less likely to watch television, because of the price of sets and the lesser availability of signals in rural areas.

A pioneering scientific audience survey for Beijing (Rogers et al. 1985) reported somewhat higher figures for media usage across the board. This may be due to the more urbanized sample and to the increase in media availability between the time our immigrants left China and 1982. However, some of the figures (such as the report that 40 percent of those with minimal literacy read a newspaper daily) lead one to suspect that some respondents may have been eager to give answers they thought would please the surveyors.

SOURCES OF INFORMATION ABOUT HONG KONG

Forty percent of the immigrants had a negative impression or no opinion at all about Hong Kong before emigrating. Only one in four came there because of a favorable impression of the colony (Table 2.3). Generally their main impression was that the city offered a higher standard of living. "I was very naive," Aw confessed. "I even asked for a job in one of the food stalls in Wanchai at a salary of $1,000 U.S. a month! Now I know that I

TABLE 2.3. Reasons for emigrating to Hong Kong

Reason	Percent
Proximity	14.5
Following others	14.5
Favorable image of Hong Kong	26.4
Relatives to depend on	44.5

Note: N = 220; multiple responses allowed.

am lucky to receive $150 a month, because I have no skills. But that is much more than I could make at home — and here I can go to school at night and eventually hope to own my own business." Similar stories are often reported in the Hong Kong press.

Most interviewees reported hearing inconsistent reports about Hong Kong, which is inevitable if they paid any attention to official channels in China. The official line was: Yes, some people make a lot of money in Hong Kong, but they have bad living conditions, are cut off from friends and relatives, have no security, and face a lawless society. Moreover, those who leave China are abandoning the Mother Country when they are needed here to work for the Four Modernizations. Respondents seemed to listen but to pay more attention to the "yes" than to the "but." They believed the official propaganda about the lack of human contact, the crime rate, and the lack of social and medical benefits in Hong Kong, but they emigrated anyway.

The immigrants' impressions of Hong Kong after they arrived were mixed (Table 2.4). "Here, everyone thinks about money all the time," one complained. "In China, the family and the Party will take care of you if you are sick or old. Rent is cheap and medicine is free, and you have many friends. In Hong Kong everything is fast and noisy and expensive. But I like it!"

We asked how the immigrants had learned about Hong Kong (Table 2.5). "Most of us have family and friends in Hong Kong," said Li Lin. "Our family and friends in China also know about the city, and we talked it over for a long time before trying to cross the border. And some people live close enough to the border to hear Hong Kong radio and television programs."

TABLE 2.4.   **Impressions of Hong Kong after arriving**

	Favorable	Neutral	Unfavorable	Unknown
Politics	20.3%	43.6%	3.8%	32.3%
Law and order	9.7	34.7	31.3	24.3
Making money	43.7	39.8	4.3	12.2
Finding jobs	42.4	45.7	4.8	7.2
Standard of living	56.8	38.1	4.3	0.8
Living conditions	10.2	39.8	33.0	17.0
Medical facilities	29.7	31.3	11.0	28.0
Education	48.3	26.3	2.1	22.3
Welfare	34.3	36.9	6.8	22.0
Human relationships	14.0	31.8	28.4	25.8

Note: N = 236.

TABLE 2.5. Sources of information about Hong Kong

Source	Used at Least Once	Rated as Most Trustworthy
Hong Kong family and friends	76.1%	58.5%
Family in China	54.8	46.5
Friends in China	64.3	44.4
Hong Kong radio and television	30.4	13.0
Hong Kong print media	1.7	2.0
Small groups	2.6	2.0
Chinese print media	14.4	0.0
Chinese electronic media	9.6	0.0

We then asked, What sources did you think were the most trustworthy? "Our family in Hong Kong," three out of five answered. Almost half relied on family and friends in China, and only 15 percent on the Hong Kong media. Only 10 to 15 percent ever used the official Chinese mass media as a source of information about Hong Kong, and none relied on them. Clearly, nonofficial channels are considered much more credible than official ones, although we did find that respondents from socially approved families were more trusting of the media, as were married individuals.

What did you do, we asked, when you found one story about Hong Kong that contradicted what you heard from another source? "We wrote to our family and friends in Hong Kong, of course," Wen replied. Almost half the sample agreed with him. A quarter of the sample talked the inconsistency over with friends, and one-fifth just ignored the conflict (Table 2.6).

FAMILY TIES

Most of our respondents had lived in a two-generation household in China, as shown by Table 2.7. The shift between China and Hong Kong reveals both a change toward one- or

TABLE 2.6. Responses to inconsistent information about Hong Kong

Response	Percent
Choose most reliable source	17.5
Talk with visitor from Hong Kong	17.5
Discuss with family	18.4
Ignore the inconsistencies	21.0
Discuss with friends	25.4
Correspond with relatives and friends in Hong Kong	47.3

Note: N = 228; multiple responses allowed.

TABLE 2.7. **Family composition**

	In China	In Hong Kong
Single individual	0.0%	12.1%
Individual + sibling or wife	5.3	43.0
Individual + either parents or child	78.1	7.5
Individual + parents and child	16.7	0.9
Individual + parents, children, and grandparents	0.0	0.0
Relatives other than nuclear family	0.0	36.4
Total	100.1%	99.9%

two-person families and toward reliance on the extended family. Whereas in China none of the respondents had lived alone or with relatives other than the nuclear family, in Hong Kong most were living alone, with one other person, or with more distant relatives.

Much of the Communist revolution has been an attempt to break up the natural cohesion of the Chinese family, replacing it with loyalty to the Party and the nation. During the Cultural Revolution it seemed that they had succeeded, at least in the cities. So we were very interested to find out how the family was holding up in China.

In important decisions, we asked, which would you choose—the alternative that would benefit your family more, or the alternative that would benefit you more personally? Many of our respondents seemed incredulous that we would even ask such a question. Three-fourths said that they would choose the family's welfare over their own.

Only 8 percent rated their family as average in its feelings of unity (Table 2.8); 70 percent said that their family was well above average when it came to sticking together. On questions of family communication the ratings dropped a bit, but still two of every three rated their family as above average. Ten percent said that their obedience to the family was below average, while

TABLE 2.8. **Importance in the Chinese family**

	Family Unity	Family Communication	Obedience to Family
Below average	0.0%	16.5%	10.5%
Average	8.5	21.2	39.5
Above average	22.0	39.0	42.1
Well above average	69.5	22.9	7.9

about two out of five said that they ranked as average or above average in minding their elders. So it is evident that the family is still the paramount institution in China. While the Party and the work unit are ultimately responsible for those who have no one, children rely on their parents for a start in life. Workers may even inherit their factory jobs from their mother or father, and young married couples need help setting up housekeeping. They may even have to share their parents' quarters or use family connections to obtain a new apartment.

On the other hand, parents still rely on children as their first defense against poverty and loneliness. Though the Party campaigns vigorously against sexism, sons are still prized as a better economic guarantee for one's old age. Female infanticide is still practiced in some regions, especially since the one-child-per-family law. Daughters tend to belong to their husband's family, though not as completely as in the old days.

INTERPERSONAL COMMUNICATION

When it comes to interpersonal communication, it is clear that our interviewees put their faith in personal contacts rather than official ones (Table 2.9). For example, in the nuclear fam-

TABLE 2.9. **Interpersonal communication**

Form	Never	Occasionally	Frequently	Very Frequently
Nuclear family	1.3%	14.9%	26.8%	57.0%
Extended family	19.1	31.4	34.0	15.5
Co-workers	13.9	17.7	36.0	32.4
Small group meetings	38.1	27.1	26.3	8.6
Political campaign meetings	44.1	29.6	14.4	11.9

ily, communication is frequent or very frequent for more than three out of four people with whom we talked, and for half of our sample in the case of the extended family. Co-workers receive the same ranking for two out of three. Only one-third of our immigrants reported frequent use of small-group meetings, and only one in four often participated in political campaigns. The nuclear family, then, especially since most of the respondents were living under the same roof as their parents, ranks very high on frequency of communication. It is not too surprising to see that our young respondents were next most likely to communicate with friends. Peer group bonds and youthful disillusionment seem as prevalent in China as elsewhere.

MASS MEDIA CREDIBILITY

We also asked each person to rate the credibility of various channels of information (Table 2.10). Some 95 percent thought that their family was either trustworthy or very trustworthy, and 80 percent ranked relatives and friends in the same manner, followed by 76 percent for foreign radio and 70 percent for co-workers.

TABLE 2.10. **Credibility ratings (percentage judging each channel trustworthy or very trustworthy)**

Channel	Percent	Channel	Percent
Family	94.9	Newspapers	46.0
Relatives	80.5	Radio	42.6
Friends	79.6	Small groups	42.6
Foreign radio	76.2	Film	38.4
Co-workers	70.3	Magazines	36.7
Wired radio	46.9	Television	33.7
		Political campaigns	28.1

Wired radio was considered trustworthy by only 47 percent, or about the same number as newspapers. Radio (not wired loudspeakers) drew 43 percent, as did small-group meetings. Films, magazines, and television rated 34 to 38 percent, and political campaigns brought up the rear with a 28 percent favorable rating.

Clearly there is a social distance scale here, with the exception of foreign radio. The closer one is to the source personally, the more credible it becomes. There may be a question of personal control as well. Wired radio is a local medium, and the audience can influence content. Even newspapers are open to letters to the editor and have a duty to investigate substantial complaints. But there is little opportunity for feedback to radio, film, magazines, and television.

Small groups and political campaign meetings, controlled

as they are by the Party, are more effective instruments for controlling the individual. "The cadres and the elders are more free to speak out in meetings," Li Lin explained. "But we all know that it can be very dangerous to do that, in case the Party line changes next year. And young people, except for some real political activists, don't like to take chances unless we really have a big stake in what's going on."

Nonofficial channels are considered much more credible than official ones. Many insisted on checking the "no opinion" category. "What do I care about whether the newspapers are lying or not?" demanded Wen. "They are the tongue of the government, and I have to read to find out what the government wants."

"If you want to get promoted inside the Party," Li Lin added, "you have to know what the government wants you to do. For instance, you need to know whether it is safe to be friendly with 'bad class' characters, or whether the Party wants you to 'Learn from Dazhai,' or to test everything by experience. When Deng Xiaopeng said, 'It does not matter whether the cat is black or gray, as long as it catches mice,' we knew that a big change was in the wind. But it is hard to follow the shifts, and so you must read the newspapers very closely."

"I think you can trust newspapers," Aw Fang said jokingly. "The news about Party directives, the scores from soccer matches, and the weather reports are pretty accurate!"

"We never put all our trust in the official channels," Wen explained. "If something important happens, we talk it over in the family and with our friends to try to decide what is true. And if the story is an international one, we can always listen to the BBC or Hong Kong radio."

This distrust of official statements was documented by a poll of Chinese young people published by *The People's Daily* in February 1981. Thirty to 40 percent of the youth have substantial doubts about the socialist system. The survey covered 900 young people in urban and rural districts of the central province of Anhui and in Fujian in the east. Thirty percent expressed doubts about socialism, even though the poll was official. Another 23.8 percent did not see that socialism was "clearly superior," and 6.4 percent flatly denied that it was superior.

The young people had widely differing ambitions. One in

four wanted to transform China into a "wealthy and prosperous nation," but two of every five did not think that the country's modernization goals could be met by the end of the century. Only 4 percent said that their ambition was to become a worker, and 1.2 percent said that their hopes had already been dashed.

Conclusions

All available evidence indicates that family influence is very high in the People's Republic, and that the mass media have little influence when these two channels of information disagree. The media and official communication channels are very important in publicizing official demands, and they have been quite influential for relatively short periods, such as during the Cultural Revolution, but this influence seems to be declining.

The decline may be due to the growing sophistication of the audience, thanks in part to travel, personal contacts, and a critical view of leadership fostered by the Cultural Revolution and by the educational programs aimed at peasants and workers. Under more normal circumstances, officials must learn to work with family interests if national goals are to be achieved.

3 MOUNTAINS, RIVERS, AND SEAS: INFLUENCE OF GEOGRAPHY ON CHINESE COMMUNICATION

"All the [geographic] world's a stage, . . ." to borrow from Shakespeare, and each [politics, economics, religion, literature, communications] must play a part.

What if England and Portugal had been as self-sufficient as China — or vice versa? If England and Portugal had not been forced into seafaring, the world might have gone unexplored for hundreds of years. If Portugal had the British economic base, her sun would not have set so quickly. Or what if the American West was no more than rock and sand? If free land and gold had not drawn men to the frontier, the North American continent might well be divided between the British, French, and Spanish, with New Englanders still pursuing whales and southerners still trading raw cotton to the British.

If China's early population had not been repeatedly decimated by disease, famine, and war, the country would surely have consolidated the conquests of Genghis Khan, at least subduing Japan, Indochina, Burma, and India. Or it might have become a great trading nation, had population outrun farmland. But this is only "what might have been." What is? How has it affected communication?

Physical geography

First, consider the size of China, especially compared to its supply of farmland. The country is slightly larger than the United States — 3,691,000 square miles versus 3,623,000 square miles. But only 12 to 15 percent of China's land is under cultivation, compared to about half of the United States, which has more than five acres of farmland for every citizen. The Chinese have about one-third of an acre per person (Pannell and Ma 1983, 118).

Roughly one-third of China is mountain country, including the world's highest and largest plateau. More than 20 percent of China soars to an altitude of more than three miles. Mountains also divide China into almost autonomous areas. Sichuan Province, for instance, roughly the size of Oklahoma, is sheltered from northern winds and northern rule by the mountains. A self-sufficient farming region with good climate and plenty of water, it often has been practically an independent kingdom. Tibet, the Tarim Pendi basin in western China, and other territories have been in the same situation (Tregear 1980, 284).

Rivers are the second most important characteristic of the Chinese landscape. They formed the only easy means of travel, especially on an east-west trek (Tregear 1980, 185). Since lines of government traditionally ran north and south, rivers were as much a hindrance as a help in centralizing power.

The country can be divided into three general regions. The eastern coast, especially toward the northern half of the country, is relatively flat, shaped by rivers that eroded the mountains and deposited vast floodplains (Pannell and Ma 1983, 30). The northwest is high, very dry, and subject to heavy wind erosion. The southwest is cold and mountainous.

Deep, rich, black soil covers Manchuria and the northeast plain, which makes up the largest area in China. The North China plain, second largest, is also covered with flat, low, sedimentary deposits, some 3,000 feet deep. To the west is the loess plateau, almost a mile high but with soil 150 to 650 feet deep. Dry and harsh, it is used only for nomadic herding and oasis farming. The eastern plain is cut in two by the Chang Jiang (the Yangtze) which has laid down deep alluvial deposits like the

Mississippi delta. Being flat, the land was often flooded (Pannell and Ma 1983, 25–36) and danger of flooding still exists. Two other rivers are important, the Huang He or Yellow River, called "China's Sorrow" because of frequent floods, and the Xi Jiang or Pearl River.

The Huang He carries an enormous load of soil from the easily eroded loess deposits, estimated at thirty-four kilograms per cubic meter. This can be compared to ten kilograms in the Colorado River and one kilogram in the Nile. Some 3,700 tons of soil wash away every year from each square kilometer in Shaanxi and Shanxi (Tregear 1980, 274). Early engineers divided the river channel and kept it dredged. Later, dikes raised the river above the surrounding farmland. Periodically the Huang He breaks loose, wiping out everything in its path.

The Xi Jiang empties into the South China Sea near Guangzhou. Its delta is the only large plain in the region and one of the richest in China.

Geography and social development

The mountainous terrain and ready access to rivers should have made seamen of the Chinese. However, there are few good harbors in the north and not much good land to generate exports in the south, which does have good harbors. Southerners did become fishermen and pirates and great fleets for war, trade, and exploration were occasionally formed; but for the most part China developed as a self-sufficient feudal agricultural estate with no desire for international commerce. While trade made some families extremely rich, it was not one of the common sources of social status or power (Tregear 1980, 198).

It is estimated that there were 100 million Chinese in the early twelfth century, but war and famine cut that to a little less than 60 million in 1381. The population grew steadily, but still was only about 401 million in 1834. The relatively small population made it easier for the peasants to support a small elite class, and it was less necessary to develop trade or industry. Succeeding waves of northern invaders were content with tribute exacted from agriculture—and, in turn, were assimilated, becoming as much Chinese as the Han, the original Chinese.

This feudal agricultural state simplified government and communication. Since practically all trading was at the local level, there was little need for a nationwide market-reporting system. Most government matters were handled locally; an annual tax satisfied the central government.

As the economic center of the country shifted to the Chang Jiang basin and further south, taxes (principally in the form of rice) had to be carried back to Beijing. Transportation changed very slowly in 2,000 years. Roads were mere footpaths occasionally paved with stone slabs. To transport goods, the south relied on men with carrying poles, wheelbarrows, sedan chairs, and boats pulled upstream by gangs of sweating laborers (Tregear 1980, 185).

Sun Yat-sen estimated that 35 percent of farm work was involved with transport, 60 percent in the mountains. He remarked, perhaps with some exaggeration, that 10,000 coolies could move 10,000 tons 170 miles in 10 days (the same load could be moved by a 5-horsepower train with 10 men in 1 day) (Lippitt 1966).

One notable exception to the lethargy in transportation development was the Grand Canal, extending about 1,000 miles from Beijing to Hangzhou. It was one of China's greatest engineering projects and the world's longest artificial waterway. Work was begun in the early fifth century B.C. and was finished at the end of the thirteenth century A.D., 1,779 years later. Its purpose was to move rice taxes north to Beijing (Pannell and Ma 1983, 166–67). As each dynasty in turn sank into decay, the canal was neglected and allowed to silt up. After the middle of the nineteenth century it was practically abandoned until the Communists reopened it in 1958.

Water in China has always been crucial and often capricious. At least 80 percent of the rain in the Huang He middle and lower basins falls in four summer months. This area has the greatest annual variation in rainfall, making it the most drought-prone area of China. Northern villages are often built around deep wells (Tregear 1980, 274).

Urban-rural geography

Except in the mountains, most Chinese live in tightly knit villages. The historic village structure was related to water and defense against bandits. Dozens of villages grew up around one small market town, connected in the past by boat or foot trails and today by rough roads.

The average northern village has 500 to 700 people. Twenty to thirty villages are served by one market town. Farmers carry their excess produce either to small markets between villages or to the market town itself. Southern villages tend to be larger, but the essential marketing pattern is the same. Southern areas may have as many as 1,500 people per square mile (Pannell and Ma 1983, 222–56). This urban-rural geography encouraged self-sufficiency and reduced the need for communication facilities in the following ways.

1. The physical and social geography of premodern China encouraged, even forced, local communication patterns—a wheel system where each participant was known to everyone in the village at least, and important people were known throughout the small market area. Villages were connected to market towns, towns to cities, and cities to the national government in a star pattern. (For a discussion of the strengths and weaknesses of wheel, star, hierarchical, political, and commercial communication systems, see Bishop 1983.)

2. Mountains and rivers made physical travel difficult, especially from north to south. Government patterns, flowing from north to south, were greatly hindered.

3. The feudal organization of agriculture made it relatively simple to assimilate each new conqueror and made for regional independence.

4. The small population and elite class plus a good climate reduced any incentive for large-scale international trade or industrialization.

5. Good southern harbors were coupled with small hinterlands, cutting down on the trade goods available. Most bulk exports would have been agricultural, but since neighboring countries were self-sufficient, large-scale trade could not de-

velop. Conversely, the richer north had few good harbors. Existing ports were always silting up, allowing only small ships to enter port and unload directly to land.

6. This weakness in seapower made China vulnerable to invasion and colonization by European seapowers. The Chinese lack of desire for imports to balance such exports as tea, led to an imbalance of trade and the Opium War (see chap. 3). Foreigners congregated in natural ports (Guangzhou, Hong Kong, Shanghai) and then extended their influence up the natural rivers. Later, railroads formed a principal avenue for Western and Japanese influence.

7. These ports became centers of modernization and revolution in the early twentieth century. In contrast to earlier agricultural revolutions, which tended to be aimed only at reform, removal of corrupt officials, and lowering agricultural taxes, later ones, which were influenced by Western thought and exploitation, intended to remodel the entire economic and political structure. Were it not for the growth of cities, education, and Western training, especially in military tactics and ideology, the 1911 Revolution would have failed, for its lines of communication and authority would have been no stronger than the existing empire.

8. Physical isolation meant social isolation. While the small intellectual elite used the same written language and even a standard dialect, each regional dialect was (and still is) almost unintelligible to other Chinese.

9. The lack of trade and industry worked against literacy; and since 95 percent of the populace did not need to read, there was little pressure to simplify the written language. Mastering the 25,000-plus characters in the Chinese vocabulary was the mark of a scholar and a barrier between classes. This is one reason for repeated attempts by the Communists to simplify the language. Many have argued that the difficulty and imprecision of the language work against scientific advancement.

10. All these factors contributed to localism or regional power, hindering national political and economic development.

Changes since 1949

When the People's Republic was founded in 1949, only a rudimentary transportation and communication system was in place. Only about 10,000 miles of railroad were functioning (Pannell and Ma 1983, 168). These ran mainly from the Trans-Siberian railroad in the north through Beijing and down to Guangzhou and Hong Kong, with branches to Shanghai and Korea and along the center of the country halfway to the western border. There was no civil aviation to speak of, since the Nationalists evacuated their few planes to Taiwan or Hong Kong. All airfields were in poor shape (Tregear 1980, 201). In 1949 the highway system included about 50,000 miles of poorly paved or dirt roads. Telecommunication was very poor, radio networking was in its infancy, and publications were an urban phenomenon.

An immediate aim was to establish the new government in every part of the country. This was to be accomplished largely through occupation by the army, although far too few trained administrators were available for the immense expansion of territory under government control.

Profiting from peace, gains from expropriated property formerly owned by "enemies of the people," and good crop yields, the government immediately began an ambitious construction program for railroads, highways, and telecommunications. The first Five-year Plan allocated 17.1 percent of total state investment capital to communications, 13.8 percent to railways, and 3.8 percent to other forms of transport (Tregear 1980, 186–97).

Railways were to be used to build a modern industrial state. They had always been built primarily north to south, supplementing the riverways, but now they were pushed into the interior as well. Industry was to be dispersed inland to ease the urban population crush, help develop the interior, and make the country less vulnerable to attack.

By 1980 it was estimated that there were about 37,000 miles of railroad in the country. Today every province or first-order administrative region is connected by rail. For comparison, India has more than 60,000 miles of railway and the United States has more than 200,000 miles.

Railroad Builders: A Shock Brigade—The army's railway corps has built one-third of China's new railroad lines, including about 240 miles of bridges and 540 miles of tunnels. Soldiers removed enough dirt and stone to build an embankment 3.3 feet high and 3.3 feet wide circling the earth 19 times (*China Pictorial* 8:1979, 3).

China now has more than four times the railroad trackage that existed in 1949. Every province is linked by rail, complemented by highways. Though the transportation system is still far short of China's needs, it has helped in unifying the country, pushing industrialization into the hinterlands, and making the country less vulnerable to attack.

Highways complement railway lines, feeding out from railhead centers to the countryside and pushing on into the most difficult terrain, such as the Tibetan plateau. The highway to Lhasa, a marvel of engineering and perseverance, is more than 13,000 feet high for 567 miles and more than 16,400 feet high for 80 miles. But Lhasa is now connected to the rail system and highways parallel the Indian border for political and military purposes (Pannell and Ma 1983, 177).

Still, reduction of official barriers to travel for the Chinese and the boom in farm and industrial production has strained railroads and roads beyond the breaking point. It is estimated that nearly 4 million people attempt to travel by rail every day on a system with a maximum capacity of 2.78 million. It is estimated that 200,000 tons of fruit and 200,000 tons of sugar were left to spoil in 1984 because of a lack of transport.

There are about 565,000 miles of roads for the entire country, but only 12,400 are said to be in first-class condition — the average speed is put at nineteen miles per hour. Civil aviation is so inadequate that 1.2 million customers were unable to get seats in 1984. Competing airlines were formed in 1985, but not enough planes are being bought or facilities built.

Rivers and canals today have doubled the mileage available in 1949. Ninety thousand miles of waterway are now navigable. Of this, 12,000 miles are open to steamships that have a draft greater than twelve feet. During the rainy season, oceangoing steamers can go up the Chang Jiang to Wuhan, more than 600 miles inland. Smaller ships, specially built for the river, can go as far as Chongqing (Pannell and Ma 1983, 166–68).

As late as 1957, telephone lines stretched only 445,000 miles. But by the early 1970s, every commune and more than 90 percent of the production brigades could be reached by phone. During the same period, mail service reached most villages.

But again, even staggering advances are dwarfed by growing needs. According to Chinese officials, postal and telecommunication service should increase by 800 percent by 2000 if demand is to be met. Even the planned 33.6 million phones would provide only one phone for every 35 people in rural areas (*Beijing Review* 1984, 7–8). The postal system, which handled 600 million letters in 1950, attempted to cope with an estimated

4 billion by 1984. Mailed copies of newspapers and magazines increased by 23 percent in 1984 over 1983 to 281 million pieces. Fights occasionally broke out between employees of the publications, who were determined to deliver their truckloads of copies to postal docks, and postal employees, who simply had nowhere left to stack the mail (*Beijing Review* 1985a, 30).

At present, only one person in 200 has a telephone, and a simple call often takes an hour to complete. Even Beijing has only 4.9 phones for every 100 people. There are not enough telephone lines, and those that exist are of low capacity and poor quality, according to *Beijing Review* (1985a, 30).

Telecommunication was greatly aided by advancing technology, though the Chinese have been rather slow in adopting advanced techniques such as satellite transmission. But microwaves and satellites make it much easier to reach remote areas. Mountains and rivers pose no great obstacle to these technologies. (Details of efforts to reach rural areas and minority groups are given in chap. 5.)

An example of the importance of rail and highway building was reported by *The China Daily* on May 30, 1985. The Xinjian Uygur Autonomous Region, in northwest China, covers one-sixth of the total country. A high desert, it has been sparsely populated and without much economic value since the beginning of humankind. But now the Chinese have verified oil deposits there of at least 1.5 billion tons. By the year 2000 production is expected to reach 20 million tons annually—about equal to the production of such minor producers as Italy, Yugoslavia, or Peru. Geologists hope to verify a new oil field equivalent in size to Daquin, a pioneer oil field in the northeast near Harbin.

They also estimate coal reserves there to be 1.6 trillion tons—just about equal to the known reserves of the United States, which has been the major source for the entire world. The Chinese estimate their total potential for hydroelectric power at 9 million kilowatts, but only about 1.7 percent is currently generated, although several hydroelectric plants are under construction.

Twenty thousand men are working to build a railroad from Urumqi, the capital, to Xinjiang on the Soviet border. The road will cost more than $230 million to complete.

Shengli Oilfields — Workers cap a gusher in the offshore oil-fields at Shengli. China, with more than 200 oilfields, is seventh in world oil production. More than 114 million tons of oil were produced in 1984 (*China Pictorial* 11:1985, 19).

Oil is a key ingredient in China's modernization, since it is badly needed for manufacturing, production of electricity, and providing transportation — all necessary for economic growth, including communication.

Geographic influences on modern communication

Geographic interference with communication has been overcome to some extent by modern technology such as improved earth-moving machinery and satellites, but China's geography still poses immense problems for transportation and communication. It has greatly influenced the amount of mass communication. Indirectly, it has been influential by determining the type and size of industries available. Probably three-fourths of the labor force is still in agriculture, usually associated with a low consumption of mass media. The urban-rural distribution of population reduces the amount of mass media available. About 80 percent of Chinese live in the countryside with limited access to any of the mass media. (The rigid system of special residence permits has avoided the ruinous rush to the cities plaguing less-developed countries, though Beijing has grown from 1 million to almost 9 million since 1949. Nanjing had about 750,000 in 1949; 3 million in 1984.)

Directly, geography affects the amount of resources available for investment, including investment in communication. Human labor has been substituted for capital investment wherever possible, probably because of the greater effectiveness of personal persuasion as well as because of a lack of facilities. Much use has been made by the government of the traveling film and theatrical and propaganda troupes. If contemporary reports of village life are credible, these are no longer particularly effective, but they were highly useful in the early stages of Mao's rule. China has rich mineral resources, including iron, coal, and oil. When properly exploited, these will have a very positive influence on communication through industrialization and an increase in gross national product.

Chinese isolation, which is at least partially geographic, tends to lessen interest in international news. But there are signs of wider interest. *Reference News,* a lightly classified government publication reprinting Western articles, circulates to a reported 11 million people. There are nightly television news programs that take a live feed from Western news agencies with a local voice-over. Lessons in English by radio are popular, as are specialized publications such as the new *World Economic Herald,* a newspaper that reprints foreign economic reports. Still, even the *Reference News* circulates to only 1 out of 100 Chinese.

Historical geography accounts for much of the survival of pre-1949 industry and arts in Shanghai, by far the most sophisticated city in China, and for the vitality of Hong Kong, China's window on the capitalistic world.

Linguistic differences affect the content, form, and distribution of communication. Although a standard dialect is being promoted today (*putonghua,* or Mandarin), it is still necessary to broadcast in each local dialect. (I was surprised to see subtitles being projected on screens to the right and left of the stage at a play given in a minority language in Beijing. But the Beijing audience needed subtitles as much as Americans do for foreign films.)

Regionalism has not faded in the years since 1949. In addition to linguistic differences, regional independence was shown by Mao's use of Shanghai as an independent base during his struggles with the Central Committee, Deng Xiaopeng's retreat to Guangzhou when he was out of favor, and the struggle over Manchuria following the Korean War. Changing political geography made an advanced, centralized communication system imperative. Central planners need accurate, quick reports from all production units. The centralization of political control and ideological indoctrination meant that the communication system had to be two-way, with mass media acting as a supplement to personal communication and control (Bishop 1983, 6–21).

4 FOUR THOUSAND YEARS OF RECORDED HISTORY: MASS MEDIA PRIOR TO 1949

Little wonder that the Chinese have always considered their land the "Middle Kingdom"—the center of the earth—and all other people as natural subjects to the mandate of heaven given to Chinese emperors. Given the world's longest continuous history, advanced scholarship, and even the invention of printing, China should have developed an advanced system to communicate across thousands of miles and between millions of people.

Unfortunately, printing and many other Chinese inventions were never put to much use. "Barbarians," as the Chinese still half-jokingly call foreigners, often reinvented or exploited ideas that the Chinese disdained, or at least did not develop.

Early media

Roswell Britton, a historian of Chinese journalism, believes that scribes probably sent news to provincial subscribers during the Han dynasty, 206 B.C. to A.D. 220, just as Roman scribes were doing at about the same time (Ko 1931; Britton 1933, 1–2). Formal court gazettes began during the Tang dynasty, 618 to 906.

Printed gazettes may date from the Sung dynasty, 960 to 1127, but certainly were seen in the Ming dynasty, 1368 to 1644. Issued by many competing publishers, the gazettes carried nothing but official court communiqués. They came in three parts. First was a sort of daily diary, listing duty officers, verbal mandates, and the emperor's calendar. Second were edicts and decrees, and third, memorials presented to the emperor (Britton 1933, 7). Past, present, and would-be officials throughout the empire eagerly read the gazettes. Merchants also followed the papers for news and amusement. They could see the funny side of court intrigues and treated the stern and dignified gazettes as comic books (Britton 1933, 12–13).

Even though movable type originated in China in the eleventh century, the gazettes were still hand carved from one block per page in the 1800s. Long press runs were printed from wooden blocks. Shorter runs used blocks of clay, gypsum, or even beeswax and resin. Sometimes colored illustrations were used (Britton 1933, 7).

The gazettes were for the intelligentsia. (Though literacy was only 3 to 5 percent, this still gave a potential audience of 10 to 20 million.) Popular broadsides were printed before 1800 for the masses, just as in Europe. These occasional papers, carrying sensational news and selling for a fraction of a cent, were called *hsin-wen-chih* or, literally, newspaper. Broadsides covered the Opium War in epic verse, illustrated by drawings of the British ships at Canton. However, the reader would never have known that China was losing (Britton 1933, 5).

Another form of Chinese communication, *tatzebao* or big character posters, is also of ancient ancestry. Posters, written secretly, were the traditional outlet for grievances against low-level officials. *Tatzebao* were formidable means of communication during the 1960s and 1970s.

Modern journalism arrived with Protestant missionaries in the early 1800s. Earlier Catholic missionaries published tracts and books but no periodicals. Protestants (who emphasized the printed word and were opposed for religious reasons by the Chinese government, the Catholic establishment in Macao, and the East India Company) turned to the printing press. Their first shop was set up in Malacca (now Melaka, Malaysia), then a major port.

William Milne, a British missionary, first published a Chinese monthly magazine in 1815. The magazine carried scientific and evangelistic articles with only a little news, but it was one of the first of what could be called revolutionary publications in China. Milne and his colleagues were introducing revolutionary technology and thought, especially by using common language rather than stilted elite phraseology (Britton 1933, 20).

Dynasty and revolution

Revolution was in the air. The Ching dynasty was declining into economic decay and social chaos, hurried on its tortuous way by foreign exploitation.

After decades of war, the population of China was estimated at only 150 million in 1700. Prosperity more than doubled the figure by 1800; but more people meant increasing pressure on economic resources, internal migration, demands on the imperial treasury, and heavier taxes on the peasants. At the end of the eighteenth century the White Lotus Rebellion, a tax rebellion led by the secret White Lotus Society, destroyed much of the emperor's authority and emptied his treasury. The silver drain caused by the opium trade and indemnities exacted by the West over the Opium War hastened the end.

The Opium War began over Britain's desire to balance her trade with China. Tea and other exports were popular in England, but the English were not selling enough to China to balance the books. Therefore, they began to import opium from India. The Chinese objected fiercely, and finally in 1839 destroyed 20,000 chests of Indian opium. The British promptly attacked and forced a ransom of $6 million for Canton, cession of Hong Kong, opening of five ports to British trade, an indemnity of $21 million, and other concessions. Other Western powers were not far behind in staking claims also.

Government exploitation of commoners continued in the form of high taxes and corrupt practices, leading to great unrest and disorder throughout the first half of the nineteenth century. But Ching nobility thought themselves immune to failure and ignored the warning signs. From 1850 until around 1880 the empire faced a series of rebellions, including the Taiping Rebellion, which went so far as to capture the important city of Nanking and to threaten Tientsin; the Nien Rebellion, which destroyed the last imperial crack army unit in 1865; and Muslim rebellions in several provinces between 1855 and 1873. These were followed by a series of droughts, especially devastating in Shansi, Shensi, and Honan provinces in 1877 to 1878.

As the century closed, the Chinese were badly defeated in the Sino-Japanese War of 1894. Aided in negotiating by Russia, Germany, and France, the Chinese gave the Russians concessions in Manchuria and the Germans concessions in Shantung Province. The British forcibly expanded their influence in the Yangtze valley, the French in three southwestern provinces, and the Japanese in Fukien Province. After abortive reforms by the boy emperor in 1898, the dowager empress again seized control and attempted to continue traditional ways.

The Boxer Rebellion began in Shantung Province in 1900 as a protest against German domination, Christianity, and starvation. The rebels besieged foreign legations in Peking on June 20, 1900, and the empress declared war on the foreigners on the twenty-first. By August 15 an international expeditionary force of 19,000 including American, British, French, Russian, German, and Japanese troops seized Peking, lifting the siege and freeing the foreigners and Chinese Christians there. Although the U.S. Open Door policy kept China from being formally carved up, independence was reduced to a polite fiction, China having to pay a large indemnity, amend commercial treaties to the advantage of foreign nations, and permit stationing of foreign troops in Peking. Thus the stage was set for modern revolutions.

Early revolutionary journalism

Models for revolutionary literature already existed in the treaty ports. Foreign powers fostered newspapers for their nationals, beginning with the *China Mail* (English) in Hong Kong in 1845 and the *North China Herald* (also English) in Shanghai in 1850. By 1931 the combined weekly and daily editions of the

Herald's successor, *The North China Daily News,* had a circulation of around 10,000. It was called the "chief foreign newspaper institution in China if not indeed in the entire Far East" (Britton 1933, 49).

The foreign-language press, including English, Portuguese, French, German, Italian, Japanese, and Russian papers, spread to the treaty ports and up the Yangtze. Casually, carelessly, the foreign "devils" fostered Chinese publications, which became the training ground for modernism and for revolutionary journalists.

The earliest modern Chinese newspaper was *Chung-wai Hsin-pao,* or the *Sino-Foreign News.* It got its start in about 1860 because the English *Hong Kong Daily Press* had a font of metallic Chinese type used for job printing. A group of Chinese set up their paper by renting the type and the *Daily Press* printing press, paying the British publisher a percentage of profits and carrying some of his ads. Britton (1933, 38) says that the arrangement continued until the Chinese paper merged with another in 1919.

The outstanding Chinese journalist in Hong Kong during this period was Wang Tao, a scholar who fled to the British colony during the Taiping Rebellion. In 1864 he became editor of the *Hong Kong News,* a Chinese-language paper sheltered by foreign ownership. Businesses owned by foreigners were exempt from Chinese law and official persecution, so Chinese papers often used foreigners as figureheads, some from good will and some for a fee. Wang went on to start *Tsun Wan Yat Pao* in 1873. The title, usually translated as the *Universal Circulating Herald,* carries more of the meaning of the inexorable evolution of natural law (Britton 1933, 43).

The paper carried edicts and memorials from the Peking gazettes and news of Canton, China, and the world. Commercial and shipping news, printed on a cheaper grade of paper than the "serious" news, took twice as much space as the rest of the paper. But it provided most of the money and, as a result, independence. Wang, an excellent writer who used the common people's language, became an influential reformer and investigative reporter, exposing corruption and giving advice to the court.

This disorganized movement came to a head in the Hundred Days of 1898, a brief moment of reform headed by the boy emperor, who was promptly imprisoned by his mother, the dowager empress. The reformers fell back on agitation, relying heavily on the printing press (Britton 1933, 98). Most reformers wrote for the intelligentsia and aristocracy in a literary language. Revolutionaries appealed to the common people in the common language. Their propaganda was so thorough that most Chinese thereafter considered agitation a normal function of periodicals. In the process, the reformers started a series of specialized publications that became the modern magazine press (Britton 1933, 98).

Reform became revolution when the court fell into sponsorship of the Boxer Rebellion, followed by the Russo-Japanese War of 1904–5, which was fought in China for Chinese territory in the face of Chinese impotency. The reformers wanted modernization under the existing government. But continued failures made the revolutionaries of 1900–11 demand the destruction of the Ching dynasty.

Sun Yat-sen, generally called the father of the Chinese Republic, was not a journalist but used journalism. In 1899 he sent Chen Shao-po to start a daily newspaper in Hong Kong. Smuggled into South China, it was Sun's first party paper. The Union of Revolutionary Leagues, founded in 1905, also published several papers.

In Shanghai, a revolutionary daily was first published in 1898 and became more and more radical until its suppression in 1903. Undaunted, the paper changed its name to the *China National Gazette* and registered under foreign ownership. *The Eastern Times,* begun in 1904 in Shanghai, was the best paper of the period. It introduced short, sharply written editorials instead of essays, in addition to a lively literary supplement. Its poetry section may mark the beginnings of publication of modern Chinese poetry (Britton 1933, 115).

Women were also revolutionary journalists. Possibly the first woman editor was Chiu Yu-fang, who was editor-publisher of *Wusih Pai-hua Pao,* published at Wusih, about eighty miles from Shanghai, in 1898. *Pai-hua,* or *putonghua,* means "common speech" or the dialect of the masses of China (Mandarin). A radical monthly magazine for women, *Nu Pao,* began in Shanghai in 1902 and was edited by Chen Chieh-fen. It was soon followed by *Women's Monthly World* and *New Woman's*

Father of the Chinese Republic — Dr. Sun Yat-sen as provisional president of the Republic, 1912 (*China Pictorial* 10:1981, 5). The Chinese finally succeeded in overthrowing the Ching dynasty in 1911, but forging a unified democratic government required desperate struggles for years. Sun died in 1925 and was succeeded by Chiang Kai-shek, commander of the National Revolutionary Army.

Chiang fought bitterly to unite the country under his own leadership, forcing the Communists to retreat to the Russian border before World War II. Following that conflict, however, his Nationalist government collapsed and retreated to Taiwan. The unity for which Sun Yat-sen fought came only under the Communists, who also revere Sun as the Father of Modern China.

World. Chiu Chin, an outstanding poet, feminist, and revolutionary, started *Chung-kuo Nu Pao* in 1906.

A daily paper edited and published entirely by women began in Peking in 1905. (*The Daily Mirror* of London began as a paper for and by women—though published by Alfred Harmsworth—a few years earlier but quickly failed.) The *Peking Nu-pao* survived for a couple of years and was followed by other dailies for women published at Peking, Tientsin, and elsewhere (Britton 1933, 116–17).

The most influential revolutionary journalist of that period is generally considered to be Liang Chi-chao (Morton 1980, 177–78). He was a follower of the great scholar Kang Yu-wei, who reinterpreted the classical writings of Confucius so as to justify the massive changes that China needed so desperately. Both men helped convince the boy emperor to institute what became the Hundred Days of Reform. When the dowager empress threw out the reform movement, Liang fled to Japan and began to publish magazines. Soon his magazines became the most powerful literary force in China. His graceful style was greatly admired by scholarly aristocrats and thus drew some of them into the reform movement (Britton 1933, 118).

Liang returned to China in 1912 after the Revolution. A founder of the Progressive party, he initially sided with Yuan Shih-kai, the general who became president of the Republic in 1912. Liang died in 1929.

The death of the Ching dynasty and birth of Chinese communism

Sun Yat-sen is the best known of the Chinese revolutionaries. Educated in Western-style schools in Hawaii and Hong Kong, he started the Revive China Society in 1894. After trying to capture Canton in 1895, he left for Tokyo, the principal center of revolutionary activities (Hsu 1983, 355–492). When the Hundred Days Reform collapsed, reformation party leaders also fled to Tokyo, where a struggle for power and funds ensued between reformers like Kang Yu-wei and Liang Chi-chao and revolutionaries like Sun Yat-sen.

The general movement was strengthened by the reluctant reforms of the dowager empress following the Boxer Rebellion. For instance, by 1905–6 there were around 8,000 Chinese students studying in Japan. Many came under the influence of reform or revolutionary groups. At the same time, Western ideas were spread through China by journals and pamphlets issued from Tokyo, Shanghai, and Hong Kong after 1900. One 1903 tract, *Revolutionary Army,* was issued in more than 1 million copies.

The intellectual ferment from so many students prompted Sun Yat-sen to rethink and elaborate his social philosophy. In 1903 he issued the prototype of his Three Principles of the People: nationalism, democracy, and socialism. After touring the United States and Europe seeking support, he was asked to head a united league of reformers and revolutionaries, although his leadership was constantly challenged.

The Russo-Japanese War raised a demand for a Chinese constitution. Beginning in 1906 the empress reluctantly modernized the government, convening provincial assemblies in October 1910. These immediately demanded a central parliament and the recovery of foreign concessionary rights. The "right-recovery" movement was mainly sponsored by the landed gentry and wealthy merchants, who had the most to gain.

Reclaiming the Hankow-Canton railroad from the American China Development Company in 1905 spurred a general railroad fever, both for recovering present rail lines and building new ones. But, unable to raise enough capital, the imperial court decided to nationalize the Hankow-Canton and Szechwan-Hankow lines in May 1911, contracting with a foreign banking consortium for finance.

When Chinese investors in the Szechwan-Hankow line set off demonstrations throughout the province, imperial troops from Hupeh occupied much of Szechwan. But some of the troops left behind suddenly mutinied and occupied Wuhan, Hupeh's capital, on October 10, 1911, a date now known as Double Ten Day and celebrated as the official start of the revolution.

Constitutional government had been nothing but an additional tax squeeze on the peasants, whose standard of living had been deteriorating since the start of the nineteenth century. Civil wars, foreign indemnities, and domestic and foreign exploitation raised the peasants' taxes to as much as twenty times the legal amount. Several peasant uprisings sputtered even before the Yangtze River flooded in 1910, sending hordes of starving people into the cities, where they became easy recruits for the revolution. In 1911 half of China was devastated by drought, adding to the desperate situation.

While the initial revolt came from Imperial troops, secret revolutionary societies quickly joined in, legitimized by several provincial assemblies that either declared independence or joined the new Republic. The strongest military group left was the nucleus of a Western-style army commanded by Yuan Shih-kai. Called out of retirement to defend the imperial government, he instead seized the powers of the court while negotiating with the revolutionaries.

Yuan turned down the presidency, apparently in hopes of establishing himself as a new emperor. Sun Yat-sen, who was serving as the provisional president, became the first president of the Republic. Yuan continued to be the most powerful man in China, and in 1913 he signed a reorganization loan with foreign powers for $125 million, dismissed three Nationalist military governors, squelched a revolt, and forced the new parliament to elect him president. Inaugurated on Double Ten Day, he dissolved parliament in January 1914 and became a dictator.

During World War I, Japan seized the German concessions in China and in 1915 presented Yuan with an ultimatum calling on China to accept the status of a Japanese dependency. However, when Yuan proceeded with his plans to become emperor, the Japanese sided with various opposition groups. By March 1915 armed revolts were splitting the country into military satrapies and Yuan was forced to renounce his plans. He died in June, leaving the country heavily burdened with foreign debt and ruled by warlords. Military dictatorship was the reality, though the Republic continued to be a glorious dream for which many revolutionaries died.

The question of declaring war on Germany set off another series of armed conflicts in 1917, including one attempt to restore the monarchy. Northern armies did publish a declaration of war in August 1917.

Sun Yat-sen attempted to set up a rival national government

in Canton, also declaring war on Germany in September 1917 and launching a northern offensive. His army was defeated by 1918, leaving a bitter split between north and south. Modernization proceeded in spite of this turmoil. By 1916 nearly 130,000 modern schools were reported in China, with more than 4 million students and 200,000 teachers. The New Culture Movement used the scientific method to analyze China's past and future. The most popular reform magazine was *New Youth,* founded by Chen Tu-hsiu in 1915. By 1917 it was the voice of the modern segment of the Peking National University faculty. By 1918 the magazine was using the common language rather than the classical style. Peking students started their own journal, *New Tide,* and scores of other groups followed (Hsu 1983, 493–501).

Revolutionary fervor was focused by protests over the Versailles Peace Treaty, giving Japan Germany's rights in Shantung. Riots and protests, now known as the May Fourth Movement, launched a new revolutionary phase. Both the Kuomintang (KMT) of Sun Yat-sen and the Chinese Communist party (CCP) sprang directly from the May Fourth Movement (Hsu 1983, 501–5).

Sun returned to Canton late in 1920 and was elected president of a new southern regime. After attempting a campaign against the north in 1922, he was driven out of the presidential residence and eventually fled to Shanghai. Returning to Canton in February 1923, he began to reorganize the Party.

The Communist party gained considerable momentum when the Russian government promised to give up all special rights and to return the Manchurian Railway. The Russians later reneged on the railroad, but they were generous compared to the Versailles Treaty and Japan. A Russian organizer, Grigory Voitinsky, arrived in 1920. Working with Li Ta-chao and Chen Tu-hsiu, he organized a Socialist Youth League. Within a year they had recruited about fifty young intellectuals, including Mao Tse-tung (Mao Zedong). The First Party Congress was held in Shanghai in July 1921, with only twelve or thirteen in attendance. By 1923 there were about 300 Party members and 3,000 to 4,000 members of the Socialist Youth League. Their railway union plans had been going badly, and in most areas it was very unsafe to be a Communist. At the urging of their Russian adviser, Maring (Hendricus Sneevliet), the Communists joined with the Kuomintang in June 1923 (Hsu 1983, 514–21).

Advised by another Russian agent, Mikhail Borodin, Sun began to draft basic national policies in preparation for the First National Congress, held in Canton in January 1924. The result was closely modeled on the Russian system. In reality, the country was split into fragments, each controlled by a local military dictator who issued his own currency, carried on his own foreign relations, and acted as the ruler of an independent country. One of Sun's goals was to bring all these petty dictators under the control of the central party, the KMT. A northern campaign succeeded in capturing Peking in the fall of 1924 when a subordinate betrayed his commander. Sun, critically ill with cancer, was invited to the capital, where he died in March 1925.

After Sun's death the Party gained some significant victories in public opinion by opposing foreign influence after a series of popular clashes with foreigners. By January 1926 the KMT reportedly had 200,000 members, while the Communists had something like 10,000.

An interparty struggle for power resulted in the ascension of Chiang Kai-shek, commander of the National Revolutionary Army. After sharply reducing the influence of the Russian and Chinese Communists, Chiang launched an expedition that captured Hunan, Hupeh, and Fukien. In March 1927 the KMT forces took Nanking and Shanghai (Hsu 1983, 527). At that point, Chiang expelled the Communists, arresting or killing many of them. The leftist faction within the KMT government was isolated and it disintegrated, leaving in power a rival conservative government formed in Nanking.

The Communists, aided by an army from Canton, attempted a series of revolts, but by the end of the year the CCP had lost most of its members, either to the sword or desertion. Forced out of central China, the Communists fought their way to the rugged southeastern region by mid-1936 (Hsu 1983, 553–63).

Growth of journalism in the early 1900s

The first third of the century saw journalistic growth accompanied by constant desperate political struggles. Lin Yutang (a European-educated Chinese scholar and journalist considered to be one of the most versatile Chinese writers of all time) reported that the number of Chinese periodicals grew from 78 in 1886 to 2,000 in 1926. There was one daily in 1886 but 628 by 1926 and 910 by 1935. Most were small, but two had circulations of more than 100,000. Counting ten readers for each copy, the daily audience reached 50 to 70 million (Lin 1936, 124, 146–49).

The journalistic style after 1900 changed also. Nineteenth-century journalists had been copyists or essayists. But between 1900 and 1912 some became reporters called *fang yuan,* literally, "inquiring gentlemen" (Britton 1933, 124, 126).

During the revolutionary period, newspapers joined the reformers' cause to drum up circulation. But after the revolution they found their new masters rather more strict than the old, weak aristocrats. Political criticism was muted in order to keep on publishing. Editors were jailed or even killed just as frequently, and foreigners were used as dummy editors even more regularly than before (Britton 1933, 124).

Lin and Britton agree that by the early 1930s there was no such thing as the power of the press, and that there was less freedom of speech or publication than at any time in the twentieth century (Lin 1936, 172). Lin quotes Edgar Snow's figure of 110 cases of suspension or suppression of publications in North China alone in 1934. Reportedly, 2,500 political prisoners lay in just one Nanking prison.

But journalistic problems were not all imposed from outside. Of the two largest papers, Lin said, "The difference between *Shun Pao* and *Sin Wan Pao* is that the *Shun Pao* is poorly edited, while the *Sin Wan Pao* is not edited at all." The one paper Lin admired had a circulation of 35,000, compared to 100,000 each for the other two. The most popular dailies, he said, were the worst edited and used news only to fill up the space around the ads. The better the paper the smaller the audience (Lin 1936, 173).

The cardinal principles of Chinese news reporting, according to Lin, were that news must be official, correct, friendly, time-tested, and untouched. It must, in other words, avoid offending anyone with power. The "mosquito press," still very active in Hong Kong, aimed at a popular audience (Lin 1936, 140):

The chief characteristics of the mosquito press, as of that particular insect, are: firstly, they bite; secondly, they swarm about; thirdly, they are hard to catch; fourthly, they don't mind little accidents, (being less important financial investments); and fifthly, they try to make an extremely annoying humming noise. But . . . in the dead silence of the big dailies respecting the most important happenings of the day, even the weak humming of mosquitoes is, to the Chinese people, a welcome relief. That accounts for the fact that mosquito papers have taken the place of the big dailies as general popular reading.

More political struggle

In the meantime, the political struggle went on between independent warlords, Nationalists, and Communists. The Nationalists expanded their base over industrial areas and seized the customs offices, a prime source of revenue. They did much to modernize the government, but the peasant's life may have grown even more desperate. At the same time, the Japanese were draining more blood from China's bruised and beaten body (Hsu 1983, 619–33).

The CCP began to call for a united front against Japan and, after being briefly imprisoned by one of his own generals, Chiang agreed to a shaky coalition. War with Japan formally began on July 7, 1937, following still another attack by the Japanese. Within a year, China lost the best of its modern armies, its air force, its arsenals, most of its industry and railroads, its sources of revenues, and all ports. The Japanese controlled cities and railroads, but no one really controlled the countryside.

The war was more or less a stalemate from 1939 to 1943. The Japanese were more interested in Southeast Asia, and neither the KMT nor the CCP could retake cities. The stalemate weakened the KMT but strengthened the Communists, who used the time to develop a unified sense of mission, learn guerrilla warfare, and mobilize the peasants. They had about 100,000 soldiers in Yenan, and by 1940 had an estimated 100,000 behind Japanese lines.

Wartime papers

War closed many papers, while others retreated to the interior. A 1942 survey by the Nationalist Ministry of Information counted 724 papers, 96 of which were run by political workers of the Nationalist army. These were mainly issued every two or three days. Periodicals numbered an additional 576 (Tong 1947, 697–703).

Wartime papers were printed in concealed country houses of mud and bamboo under thatched roofs or in dugouts. Many were bombed out several times. They printed on any paper available, mostly *chia-lo,* paper like brown grocery sacks, using wood blocks for type. Four pages was their size limit, and sometimes political enemies had to share the same sheets, one on the front and one on the back. In the villages and behind Japanese lines, wall papers, big character posters, and mimeographed newspapers carried on. The Nationalist army had eleven newspapers by 1942 and its own correspondents corps, called *Chien Pao Pan* or Flash News Corps. Fifty units provided news and propaganda to troops and civilians.

Tying the papers together were radio broadcasts by the Central News Agency (CNA), started in 1924. The early CNA was an official branch of the KMT. T. T. Hsiao became director in 1931 and established a national network of correspondents and radio stations for collecting and disseminating news. The agency broadcast news bulletins at dictation speed to isolated papers, even many behind Japanese lines (Tong 1947, 700, 702).

The American Office of War Information (OWI) was very active in Chungking and behind enemy lines. One OWI director, John C. Caldwell, once traveled for twenty-four days in "occupied territory," inspecting twenty newspaper plants and speaking

Young Revolutionary — Mao Zedong, pictured in 1921 (*China Pictorial* 7:1981, 1). Mao was one of the founders of the Chinese Communist party at the beginning of the 1920s. After several shifts in power, he took command of the remnants of the Long March (the Communist retreat from southeast China to Yenan on the Russian border). Mao and his group successfully reorganized both the Communist party and the People's Liberation Army so as to win the backing of the peasants and eventually to overthrow the Nationalist government. The People's Republic of China was proclaimed in 1949.

Mao is revered for his work in establishing the People's Republic. His mistakes in trying to promote instant modernization through the Great Leap Forward and in trying to perpetuate revolutionary zeal through the Cultural Revolution are now acknowledged. Still, he is considered the most important figure in modern Chinese history.

to 50,000 people in mass rallies. He reported that 135 daily newspapers were publishing in the coastal region, which was in fact controlled by Chinese pirates rather than the Japanese. Of the 135, only 7 had no official connection with some political party (Bishop 1966, 277–307).

At the end of May 1945, some 1,848 magazines and periodicals were reportedly being published in Nationalist areas. Chungking, the wartime capital, headed the list with 527. Military units sponsored 300. Most periodicals were monthly.

Early Communist communication

When the CCP was founded in 1921, Li Ta was put in charge of propaganda, but he had no mass media to use. The propaganda department gained stature under Peng Shu-shih in 1924 but did not control Party newspapers.

Hsiang-tao, or *Weekly Guide,* founded soon after 1924, is the earliest forerunner of *The People's Daily,* although it does not trace its own lineage back past 1946. Tsai Ho-sen and Chu Chiu-pai edited the *Guide.* Other early periodicals include the *Hsiang River Review,* edited by Mao Tse-tung, and *New Youth,* edited by Chen Tu-hsiu (Yu 1979, 28–29).

Early years of Mao Tse-tung

These early years, called the First Revolutionary Civil War, solidified Mao's ideas about revolution and communication. Born a member of the small landlord class in 1893, Mao was a secondary leader of the CCP until 1927, when he began to organize peasant rebellions in south central China. After Chiang Kai-shek destroyed the CCP in the cities, Mao had the only effective Communist army and assumed leadership over Moscow's objections (Daniels 1962, 290).

His report to the Central Committee, "The Struggle in the Chingkang Mountains," laid out the requirements for success:

popular support, strong party organization, an adequate army, favorable terrain, and economic strength. He explicitly credited the strength of the Red Army to political education. Every soldier learned about class warfare, land redistribution, and the other Party aims. The army was a democracy — officers and men were treated equally, there were no beatings or mistreatment, and account books were open to anyone.

Mao was well aware that revolutionary fervor was dying down in 1927 and that he had to enlist both peasants and urban workers. "We have an acute sense of loneliness," he said, "and are every moment longing for the end of such a lonely life. To turn the revolution into a seething, surging tide all over the country, it is necessary to launch a political and economic struggle for democracy involving also the urban petty bourgeoisie."

Other important ideas — such as the use of simple slogans, peasants' associations, mass meetings, and attacks on landlords — were laid out in Mao's "Report on the Investigation of the Peasants' Movement in Hunan" in March 1927 (Mao 1954, 71, 79–83, 99).

From 1928 to 1934, the Nationalists forced the Communists to retreat to Kiangsi, where the first Chinese soviet was formed. The retreat gave them time to reform the army and to try out ideological education. The First All-China Congress of Soviets established the Chinese Soviet Republic on November 7, 1931, with Mao as chairman (Yu 1979, 31).

The Communists defeated the Nationalists in four successive campaigns between 1930 and 1934, only to fail in the fifth assault when Chiang surrounded the Communists with cement blockhouses. Mao had been demoted in early 1934, and his guerrilla tactics were abandoned for conventional warfare against the bigger, better-armed Nationalist armies. Crushed, the remaining 100,000 Communists broke out on October 15, 1934, and began an incredible yearlong march covering 6,000 miles, eighteen mountain ranges, and twenty-four rivers to the Russian border. This epic struggle became known as the Long March and is perhaps the most important of Chinese Communist symbols.

Under constant attack, 8,000 survivors, again commanded by Mao, reached Shensi Province in October 1935. In December 1936 they moved to Yenan for the remainder of the war, fighting both Japanese and Nationalists. (Other elements, arriving later, brought the number of survivors to around 30,000.)

Hung-se Chung-hua, or *Red China,* began within a month after the establishment of the Chinese Soviet Republic, first as a weekly and then on a three-day schedule. It reported a circulation of 50,000 by 1934. *Tou-cheng,* or *Struggle,* began in 1933 after the merger of two official newspapers, *Plain Talk* and *Party Construction. Struggle* became the official organ of the Central Bureau of the CCP. The army started its own paper, *Hung Hsin,* or *Red Star,* in 1933. The New China News Agency, or Xinhua, was organized by Mao in 1931 and accompanied the army on the Long March to Yenan.

Communication under Mao

The third period of Communist history, 1936–1949, was marked by full-scale warfare against the KMT and the Japanese and a rebuilding of the Party. Criticism and self-criticism sessions were introduced, along with demanding study programs (Liu 1939, 336, 343–44).

The first major Party rectification campaign was *Cheng Feng,* or Ideological Remolding Campaign, of 1942, which established central control on the Russian model under Mao's leadership. Principles of mass manipulation and Party control over thought and culture were firmly established (Daniels 1962, 312; Yu 1979, 32).

The campaign began with essays written by Communist leaders, especially Mao himself. But newspapers, magazines, wall posters, and every conceivable form of persuasion were used, including intense "struggle" sessions to brainwash dissidents. Mao seriously tried to consolidate control, weeding out rival ideologies and experimenting with thought reform. He saw the control of intellectuals and bourgeoisie as central to controlling the country.

Several publications were started to purify and unite the Party. *Kung Chan Tang,* or *Communist,* was a special study journal for Party members and cadres. *Chung-kuo Kungjen,* or *Chinese Workers,* was aimed at the working classes. The official

Party organ was *Hsin Chung-hua Pao,* or *New China Daily,* which became *Chieh-fang Jihpao,* or *Liberation Daily,* and was published until spring 1949, when Yenan fell to the KMT.

The immediate ancestor of *The People's Daily* was a two-page paper in Hopeh in 1946. Two years later, *The People's Daily* merged with the *Shansi-Chahar-Hopeh Daily.* The merged paper kept the name of *The People's Daily* and moved to Peking in 1949. It is today the official paper of the Central Committee of the CCP (Yu 1979, 37).

The Party worked hard and effectively during World War II to educate the people, both in literacy and politics. The Communists ran literacy classes, winter schools, people's schools, people's blackboards (a form of newspaper), newspaper reading groups, people's revolutionary recreation rooms, and rural theater groups. Even outside Yenan they had some influence. Their coalition with the KMT allowed several editions of the *New China Daily News* to publish in KMT territory, directed by Chou En-lai.

RADIO BROADCASTING

Radio broadcasting began in 1940 with a Russian transmitter and scavenged parts. The Yenan Hsin Hua broadcasting station had one old manual record player. Mao reportedly donated twenty of his own records to the station, which often operated out of caves and half-destroyed buildings under extremely difficult conditions. Radio probably was used more to keep in touch with liberated areas, the army, and guerrillas. Not yet a principal propaganda tool—there were very few receivers in all China—it became a major weapon immediately after 1949, when the Communists swept to victory (Yu 1979, 37–38).

ART AND LITERATURE

The Party had at least two and perhaps three main groups working in art and literature. One, led by Mao, was in the countryside. Another was in the KMT-controlled urban areas, out of touch with peasants and soldiers. The third was a cultural workers corps with the army, which grew rapidly between 1945 and 1949. These three are still in conflict.

Mao preached that all art, regardless of artistic merit, must serve the revolution — following a line similar to that of the Soviet Union. But some always saw merit in traditional art — just as the Russians have preserved ballet, one of the world's great collections of Picasso and the Dutch masters, and classical music. (Some ballet has been recast into propaganda and musicians are often pressured to conform, but somehow these traditional arts have survived.)

5 THE PEOPLE'S REPUBLIC AFTER 1949

The People's Republic of China, officially proclaimed on October 1, 1949, faced massive problems that only industrialization could solve. Obviously a rural-based movement was not sufficient, but Mao insisted on the efficacy of his rural-based ideology (Hsu 1983, 645–52). Establishing control was his first goal.

In a series of speeches in 1949, Mao announced his aim of creating socialism in China and eventually the world. Consumer cities would be made over into producer cities, and on these the people's political power would build. The chairman acknowledged that the state had to be strengthened temporarily "for the defense of the nation and protection of the people's interests."

Nominally, the new government was a coalition of bourgeoisie, workers, and peasants led by the Communist party. For this reason at least three newspapers that had leftist leanings but no Communist affiliations were allowed to continue publishing. Also left standing was a shell representing "democratic" but non-Communist political parties.

The Communists sincerely believed that all Chinese would

From this point on we will use the modern, or *pinyin,* transliteration of Chinese words, except where the person involved uses the Wade-Giles plan.

A Youthful Mao Zedong and Zhou En-lai — Mao was the charismatic leader, Zhou the wise adviser. Mao always "stormed the heights," attempting to achieve his goals by human wave assaults on any obstacle, whether military, political, or economic. Zhou interpreted West to East and mediated between revolution and education. He was practically the only adviser whose loyalty was never seriously doubted by Mao, even when he urged moderation at the height of the Cultural Revolution (*China Pictorial* 1:1977, 3).

Premier Zhou En-lai — With the establishment of the People's Republic of China in 1949, Zhou became premier and foreign minister. He was China's face to the West for decades, her best-known diplomat, and an influence for moderation and modernization. Beloved by the Chinese people, it was the disrespect shown to his memory by the Gang of Four that seemed to be the immediate cause for their arrest and China's shift from revolutionary fanaticism to economic and political reform under Deng Xiaoping (*China Pictorial* 1:1977, cover).

unite, acknowledging that their interests were best expressed by the Communist party. Then the state could wither away. Presumably they ignored the example of the Soviet Union or blamed persistent problems on World War II and capitalistic encirclement.

Exhausted and desperate, China quickly accepted the "new order." Practically all industrial production had stopped and only local goods were available, since transportation was at best sporadic. Sometimes not even water and electricity were available. Anything was better than starvation and disease, and many welcomed the new order. Certainly, poor peasants saw the promise of land redistribution.

To get the economy running, however, the Communists had to use Nationalist bureaucrats and capitalistic factory owners, foremen, and teachers, for they had no replacements. Then the spoils system set in. Party and army members looked for rewards in political posts. They could no longer condone the contempt for government that they once sponsored. "Careerism" dominated many cadres and young people who saw that the traditional advantages of education and family connections were still important, even to Communists.

A revolutionary, even messianic, movement was institutionalized, a process that history has shown always threatens putrefaction if not petrifaction as a result. Idealistic, evangelical Communists were dismayed, and another fault line began to run through the Party.

The Korean War (1950–1955)

Militant spirits were kept alive between 1949 and 1952 by real and imagined foreign dangers. In October 1950 the Chinese believed that the United Nations forces then pushing toward the North Korean border might well attack China. After several warnings, Chinese "volunteers" in North Korea joined the fight. When the war settled down to a stalemate in July 1953 as a result of their effort, the Chinese felt a surge of national pride as an armistice was signed. At the same time, they distrusted the Russians, whose support had been grudging and expensive.

COMMUNICATIONS

In China a "Resist America, Aid Korea" campaign aroused patriotic feelings and excused economic shortages and government flaws. Threats from Taiwan justified "Regulations for the Suppression of Counterrevolutionaries" and campaigns against anti-Communists, bandits, and political opponents.

Mobilization for war centralizes power. As quickly as possible, non-Communist holdovers were ousted from office, school, and factory. Two major urban campaigns were the "Three Anti-" campaign within the government against corruption, waste, and bureaucratism and a "Five Anti-" campaign against bribery, tax evasion, stealing state property, stealing state secrets, and cheating on government contracts.

The Party's main job was to establish the new government's authority and to build new political attitudes. One of the tools was radio, used in all the mass campaigns and in broadcasting "bad element" trials. Because there were relatively few radio receivers, groups listened together in factories and villages.

One report, reprinted from the *New China Monthly* by Liu (1975, 122) says that only about 2 million people listened to reports from Chinese volunteers in Korea. Probably most were in the cities, as a survey for another campaign reported 1.18 million organized listeners in Beijing, Nanjing, Chongqing, and Jinan.

Newspapers pushed Party organization by transmitting Party instructions (crucial, since the scope of administration had expanded so quickly) and published both self-criticism and concrete criticism of local Party activities. Worker-correspondents were recruited, trained, and organized—all to strengthen the identification between the masses and the Party (Liu 1975, 136).

In the book publishing realm, Liu's analysis of the *Chinese National Bibliography* indicates that most books published between 1949 and 1952 dealt with ideology, world communism, and mass campaigns in China. The books had a dual purpose: to educate the masses about communism (through being read aloud and discussed in groups) and to encourage activists. Liu (1975, 150, 154) concluded that collective book reading was haphazard in the countryside, and ineffective in the cities. Regional publishing houses were opened, only to be accused of undermining centralism. It was felt that they helped remind readers of the cultural heritage, literature, and history of separate regions. Several efforts were made to fulfill campaign promises. First, the Agrarian Reform Law of 1950 gave land to peasants. Second, the Marriage Law of 1950 broke cleanly with old customs. Men and women were freed from arranged marriages, bride price, and bans on divorce and the remarriage of widows. (However, the old customs linger, especially in the country. Even now, most marriages are arranged, but with the couple's consent.) And third, mass organizations were formed for economic, social, and demographic groups — labor unions, peasant organizations, youth groups, women's clubs, and so on. These were heavily involved in mass campaigns and mass education for the Party.

But the Korean War also fostered China's old nemesis, independent fiefdoms, especially Manchuria. Kao Kang, who coordinated Party, army, government, and industry in the northeast, became especially powerful. An advocate of Soviet-style industrial planning, he and Jao Shu-shih, chairman of the East China Military and Administrative Committee, apparently tried to take over in 1953. Among those threatened were Liu Shaoqi and Deng Xiaoping (Hsu 1983, 651, 654, 663).

The power struggle lasted for a year, with the mass media emphasizing Party unity and discipline until Kao and Jao were crushed. Liu Shaoqi then became second in command to Mao. As a result of this power struggle, Russia's grudging support of the Korean War, and a fundamental difference in national interests, Soviet influence gradually began to decline (Hsu 1983, 673–89).

Nevertheless, Soviet political propaganda materials inundated the country and Soviet equipment and aid continued to be vital, especially for the army. The USSR was the unquestioned leader of international communism, strongly influencing Chinese foreign policy.

Postwar development (1955–1958)

Once the Korean War was over and Communist authority established, the emphasis switched to development. For the media, the watchword was mass education rather than agitation

(Liu 1975, 121–22). Radio listening groups diminished and entertainment, including Western classical music, was heard again (Liu 1975, 122).

Newspapers were given a new charter, promoting a new Five-year Plan. This plan, implemented between 1953 and 1957, emphasized quick-step industrialization through rural collectives, heavy industry, and exploitation of natural resources (Hsu 1983, 645–64). The newspapers were urged to tell about economic successes, always putting the facts into the proper context, that is, any gains in production stemmed from Communist ideology (Liu 1975, 136–37).

Book publishing fell into line, with less emphasis on ideology and more on science and technology. Between 1949 and 1955, 3,400 foreign science and technology books were published. Two-thirds were from the Soviet Union (Liu 1975, 150–51). Since patriotism and nationalism were needed to motivate industrialization, many Chinese classics were reprinted, especially after 1955.

The devastated film industry was reorganized between 1953 and 1957. Three main centers were resuscitated: Changchun, Beijing, and Shanghai. Changchun specialized in dubbing Chinese into Soviet films, Beijing handled feature films and newsreels, and Shanghai did education and science films, cartoons, and some dubbing. Later, because of cultural differences between these urban areas and the rest of the country, studios were built in Xian and Guangzhou. In order to penetrate the entire country with radical propaganda, the Party decided in 1958 to build newsreel and documentary studios in every province. Film content followed the same general lines as the other media: nationalism, patriotism, industrial development. Documentaries carried accounts of classical art, monuments, and scenery from all over China. Film personnel had been terrorized by the early campaigns to reform intellectuals, but political control loosened somewhat in 1953 to allow feature films (Liu 1975, 158–60).

Forcing the organization of rural collectives was both circuitous and deceptive. First, peasants were given land of their own in 1949. Then, in 1951–53, teams of neighbors were formed for mutual aid—an ancient practice. But in 1953 the voluntary mutual-aid teams were transformed into small collectives. The farmer still owned his land, and at least in principle could quit the collective whenever he chose. Farmers split the profits based on their land and their labor. Some were unhappy, but most agreed that larger farms were easier to work and more profitable for everyone.

In the fall of 1955, however, the Party took another step: It created large communes. The farmer lost his land and was paid only for his family's labor. At the same time, the Party became the landlord, taxing away much of the crop, sometimes even when there was not enough produce to support the commune. It was the only way to finance industrialization, but many peasants were worse off than under the old regime (Hsu 1983, 652–58).

Farmers' resistance started a bitter debate, but Mao remained firm, insisting on a "high tide of socialism in the countryside" and collectivization of business and industry. By the beginning of 1957, 88 percent of peasant households were in large cooperatives. Attracted by city life and repelled by the farmer's unrelenting labor and apparent hopelessness, Chinese moved to town by the millions. The urban population almost doubled in eight years, from 77 million in 1953 to 130 million in 1961.

Careerism, that old specter, appeared once more. Young people thought less about the glorious revolution than about getting ahead through education, the Party bureaucracy, or personal influence. Morath and Miller (1979, 86) report a 1978 conversation with the vice-chairman of Guilin's Revolutionary Council:

"In the early days of the revolution," he said, not quite meeting my gaze, "there was a fine tradition of democracy here. The people—all of them—would vote about everything. They were almost all illiterate, but there were bowls set out and they would drop in black or white beans to vote yes or no on rival issues and candidates. And there is something else."

Su Guang, who was translating, showed a certain excitement in his eyes which was hard to interpret as either surprise at this official being so confessionally candid, or else his own fear of the discussion spilling over its proper limits.

"To be a cadre now has become a profession. It used to be a vocation, work that one did because one felt called to it and to the sacrifices it entailed. A cadre was not the first to be fed but the last, not the first to get living space but the last, and he drank from the bottom of the cup not the top. To be a cadre was not an honor then, it was a walk into the direct line of fire. More than likely, in fact, the people you were trying to help would not understand, at least not all of them, and would distrust you and even hate you. To be a cadre, you see, was not a profession in those times."

Mao's closest lieutenants worried that the revolution would be wiped out by city young people and intellectuals (an intellectual meant anyone with a high school education). At the same time, officials were threatened by the disillusionment of the peasants and rural youth, the Party's backbone. Once Party members had been soldiers and peasants. Now millions joined, 11.7 percent were intellectuals. (Party membership passed 17 million in 1961 — almost four times the size of the 1949 Party.)

In early 1956 an overconfident Mao launched the Hundred Flowers campaign, encouraging free discussion. The name came from Mao's phrase, "Let a hundred flowers bloom," which seemed to mean that opposing viewpoints could add color to the gray Marxist landscape. His libertarian assumption seemed to be that Marxism-Leninism would inevitably win in any free discussion. *The People's Daily* engaged in a long self-criticism, announced that it would publish opinions not necessarily approved by the editors, and promised to promote free discussion of policy. Intellectuals unwisely began to criticize Communist theory and leadership and debate Western ideas (Hsu 1983, 663–64). By June of 1957 Mao's extremely vulnerable critics had fallen into a deadly trap and the Hundred Flowers movement was relentlessly cut down by an antirightist campaign.

The Great Leap Forward (1958–1960)

Because the first Five-year Plan had been so successful, Mao and the Chinese leadership abandoned Soviet-style industrialization for the "human sea" of the 1958 Great Leap Forward, which was an economic program aimed at making

China a major industrial power overnight. It was believed that political fanaticism and millions of hands would accomplish in a few months what other countries had taken decades to do.

Life became one long mass campaign. Workers and peasants alike spent most of their time in study programs and "speak bitterness" meetings designed to heighten class warfare. Traditional drama and operas were rewritten on the new political line and staged by small traveling troupes of young people (Hsu 1983, 691–93).

The "revolutionary purity of the peasant" seemed to hypnotize Mao's followers. Every effort was made to shift economic production, including factories, smelters, and marketing to the countryside. One reason was to keep young people on the farm by enriching the country. Part of this delusion was a naive romantic belief in the innate goodness and wisdom of the farmer versus the unnatural life of city people. But Mao also recognized that the Party's support was in the country, while most opposition was urban.

A first step was to form large, self-sufficient, rural communes, growing their own food and providing marketing, schools, public administration, and local police and militia. Some 24,000 communes were set up, each averaging 5,000 households. These cut across kinship and village lines, attempting to impose new loyalties to replace family ties.

The reorganization was strongly resisted. Competent managers could not be found for so many large enterprises; family tradition was against communes, and some projects, such as backyard foundries, were simply unworkable. On top of that, the country had four hard years of severe drought, with mass starvation in some areas. Estimates of famine deaths ranged from an official Chinese figure of 10 million to American estimates of 30 million (*Atlanta Journal-Constitution* 1984). Riots and even rebellions broke out. Romanticism had to yield to reality.

The leadership publicly blamed bad weather, low-level officials, and the Soviet Union (which pulled out its technicians sent under the first Five-year Plan) for their failures. But, pragmatically, they began to back down, eventually reorganizing into production teams of twenty to thirty households.

MEDIA

The media were thoroughly mobilized to promote the Great Leap Forward, with special attention to rural communication. For example, only 90,500 rural loudspeakers for wired radio were reported in 1955. By 1959 the reported figure was 4.57 million. Even if the actual number was half that, the leap was tremendous. Less successful were county newspapers, which faced a number of difficulties. Liu (1975, 120, 132, 135) estimates that 1,000 were set up, but they foundered for want of machinery, supplies, trained personnel, and, most important, literate readers. By 1963 county and commune papers had been replaced by special provincial editions.

Wired radio systems were set up with transmitter-receivers in the county seat and receivers in most villages. Powerful loudspeakers dominated all public places, making it almost impossible to escape the din in the city. In villages, speakers blatted early in the morning before field work began and again in the evening. Programming varied according to the ability of local broadcasters. The county radio got about half of its material from Beijing and originated half. This allowed translations into the local dialect (some eighteen dialects were necessary) and some local adaptation. Some villages also carried local material (Liu 1975, 123; Chan et al. 1984, 84–87).

Programming took a nationalistic turn, with Western influences banned. Scorning intellectualism, the main propaganda themes glorified the military—the soldier's role in national development. Soldiers were pictured as unselfish, persistent under hardship, and unswerving in Party beliefs.

The radical left, firmly in control, began an antiprofessional drive against media staffs. (One must remember that top staff members were Party members first and journalists second, if at all. Most lower-level journalists desperately wanted to become Party members and would never contradict the latest Party doctrine.) Newspapers became even more propagandistic, carrying little domestic news except reports of glorious achievements through Mao's thought (Liu 1975, 137–38).

Book publishers reverted to politics and ideology. Simple political tracts aimed at the masses were printed by the millions. Films were greatly simplified, and most production turned to newsreels and documentaries featuring the current political campaigns (Liu 1975, 151–52, 160–61).

Return to reality (1960–1962)

In 1959 Mao turned over major responsibilities to Liu Shaoqi and Deng Xiaoping to devote himself to fundamental policy and philosophy, possibly recognizing the Great Leap Forward's failures. But the public explanation was that Mao's superior policy had been sabotaged by incompetents and enemies of the people. Before long the chairman decided that even his successors were Soviet-style revisionists and were killing his great dream. Mao's role in the Great Disaster did not go unnoticed. After 1962, essays attacking his competence were published openly, which suggests that the authors relied on high officials for protection. They would not have risked another Hundred Flowers!

The media again switched course as the more pragmatic elements of Party leadership took control. As a result, agitation disappeared and traditional authority figures such as parents and teachers were prominent, apparently to reinforce Party authority and public obedience. From 1963 until 1965, and during the Cultural Revolution, newspapers balanced industrial propaganda and mass ideology. Attacks on the Soviet Union and other Communist countries often made up all the national and international coverage, while domestic stories featured military heroes (Liu 1975, 138).

Disappointed in the peasantry, Mao turned to the People's Liberation Army and the sycophantic Lin Biao. Lin purged army dissidents, reestablished central military control, and began Mao's deification. Victories in brief battles on the Indian border in 1962 helped restore army discipline and prestige and popularized military heroes for mass campaigns again.

Broadcasting between 1961 and 1966 seems to have reverted to the policies of 1953–57, catering to popular taste and coating propaganda with entertainment. Feature films came back and writers were allowed to use "middle-position" characters –

neither pure hero nor pure villain. But there was a new emphasis on scientific and educational films for the countryside (Liu 1975, 124, 161).

Radical resurgence and the Cultural Revolution (1963–1973)

The Cuban missile crisis and Russian neutrality in the Sino-Indian War set off hot denunciations of the "timid capitulators" of the Soviet Union. The partial nuclear test ban of 1963 sent the Chinese on a nationalistic binge and strengthened the army.

Intellectuals were mobilized to support the new Party line of self-sufficiency and international destiny. Mao's 1964 essay, "On Khrushchev's Phoney Communism and Its Historical Lessons for the World," became the text for educating young revolutionaries. But American air strikes on North Vietnam were seen as menacing and dampened expansionist fever. For a year the Party debated the wisdom of disruptive political campaigns in the face of external threats. The debate was whether China should get ready for an immediate conventional war with the United States or continue to revolutionize Chinese society as Mao demanded.

Defection from Mao's authority was troublesome. The non-Maoist factions continued to reduce rural collectives, allowing a limited free market system and private ownership of garden plots. Maoists denounced these "corrupt" liberalizations, and in January 1965, for the first time, Mao charged that China's main enemies were inside the Communist party. Again, he urged class struggle and campaigns to "educate" the masses into the Party line.

Convinced that the 1964 "reforms" had been deliberately sabotaged, Mao and Lin led a purge of army and Party leaders, beginning in September 1965, leading to the Cultural Revolution, which began with the People's Liberation Army but eventually spread to every village. In the beginning, Mao's base was in Shanghai, and his standard-bearer among newspapers was the *Liberation Daily*. But his main propaganda apparatus was the army, which promoted Mao's thought through the famous little red book, *Quotations from Chairman Mao Tse-tung* (a cross between a rabbit's foot and a Crusader's cross), and control of central broadcasting, its own newspapers, and propaganda teams. The army held ultimate political power as well.

MEDIA

Young Chinese were targeted for motivation in Mao's cause. Using mass media, national organizations, the telephone network, the army—every resource—the Maoists called young people to Beijing to meet Chairman Mao. Eight emotional demonstrations filled the capital between August 18 and November 26, 1966. Millions of youngsters calling themselves Red Guards came by train, bus, or foot, setting off local rebellions in every town as they passed. Their principal communications medium was the big character poster, each group "proving" its own purity and denouncing apostate rivals. Big character posters first appeared on Beijing university campuses. University teachers and administrators were bitterly attacked. Students held mass meetings to organize for struggles against real or imagined enemies. Although Mao resigned as chairman of the People's Republic during the failures of the Great Leap Forward, he had gained control of the Central Committee by August 1966 and issued his own big character poster, "Bombard the Headquarters." It, plus a Central Committee report, called for seizing power from bourgeois elements, especially in cities. Liang and Shapiro (1983) have written an affecting memoir on growing up Communist.

Cultural Revolution broadcasting became extremely propagandistic, strident, and chauvinistic under the direction of Mao's wife, Jiang Qing. Entertainment was limited to revolutionary songs and dances, especially the eight model operas she approved. Prudent local stations often stopped carrying anything but rebroadcasts from Beijing or programs such as "Workers, Peasants, and Soldiers Learn Chairman Mao's Works."

Newspapers, taken over first by one group of leftists and then by another, generally played it safe by echoing papers published by the army or the Gang of Four, as Mao's wife and her cronies came to be called (Liu 1975, 123–25; Liang and Shapiro

1983 — Liang's father was a journalist purged from Changsha).

The leader of the Gang of Four was Jiang Qing, a minor Shanghai actress who became Mao's second wife in 1940. She stayed in the background for twenty years, allegedly because the Party made that a condition of approving the match. But Mao gave her some general power over Chinese cultural life in the early 1960s, and her influence grew enormously throughout the Cultural Revolution. Mao was not active in Party affairs during the last years of his life, and it is thought that much of what was issued under his name was inspired by or even completely the work of Jiang Qing. The second member of the gang was Yao Wenyuan, their specialist in Maoist thought. Zhang Chunqiao, the third member, was a senior member of the Xinhua News Agency and became chairman of Shanghai's revolutionary committee in 1967. Fourth was Wang Hongwen, who became vice-chairman of the Party in 1973.

The short-lived liberalization of films in 1961–63 came under strident attack. The reason may have been that Jiang Qing had once been an actress and wished to persecute those who had slighted her or even knew of her checkered past. Soon only paper heroes and cardboard villains were allowed. Feature films were pretty much confined to the eight model operas plus newsreels and documentaries about the Red Guard.

Great efforts were made to show more films in the villages, though many were not in the local dialect and had to be translated by the operator. Early in the Cultural Revolution local work brigades were required to pay as much as a man's monthly wage for each showing. Later, political films were free (Barnett 1967; Liang and Shapiro 1983).

POLITICS

Following the national demonstrations, Mao called for power seizures in every city. These struggles, which sometimes deteriorated into riots and even battles with artillery, machine guns, grenades, and rockets, seemed to hinge on local issues, masked by the hysteria of an incredible Children's Crusade (described in chap. 6) (Liang and Shapiro 1983, 128–37).

Urban survivalists had to participate in every meeting, study group, poster campaign, reenactment of the Long March, or denunciation of enemies of the people. Some peasants were relatively unaffected, except for having to feed hordes of long marchers and having to put up with exiled city dwellers. Others were torn apart emotionally by teams of outsiders or by urban youth sent down to the countryside to learn from the peasants. Practically all production stopped for months, and few were foolish enough to accept positions of leadership. In the long run, the Chinese were deeply disillusioned with Maoism.

Mao's underlying motive was not so much to get rid of individuals, although plenty of old scores were settled, but to stop the growth of bureaucracy and to rekindle the participatory democracy of Yenan present after the Long March. The leftists confidently expected that utopian perpetual revolution would come out of chaos. But the army, ordered to overthrow existing order, merely imposed its own. It quickly filled key positions in broadcasting, newspapers, transportation, telecommunications, Party, and state. National defense sectors, granaries, and arsenals were protected from peasants and Red Guards alike.

Civilian government was more or less replaced by revolutionary committees, a three-way alliance of soldiers, leftist cadres, and the revolutionary masses. With so much disorder, these two forces—the revolutionary committees and the army—tended to localism, even resisting Beijing. By the winter of 1967, the Central Committee began to try to restrain anarchism.

At the same time, however, public campaigns to discredit Liu Shaoqi, Deng Xiaoping, and others removed in 1966 sparked similar actions throughout China, resulting in a wave of terror. Red Guards within Chinese communities and Chinese embassies in foreign capitals rioted, attacking their own officials and the British of Hong Kong. The rioting peaked in Wuhan, when major army units had to be sent in. Millions of young Chinese roamed city streets, claiming messianic authority from Chairman Mao.

After a secret trip to inspect some of the worst areas, Mao backed off. To remedy the situation, in October the Central Committee urgently drafted youths, sending them to some of the most inhospitable parts of the country. The government bureaucracy was reduced to one-sixth its previous size. Thousands of displaced or disgraced cadres were also dumped in the country.

By 1968 the country began to regain its composure, but wrecking the educational system continued. Admittance to high school, vocational schools, or college depended on how fervent your communism was, not on whether you could pass a literacy test. The same was true for teachers. Little was taught; less learned.

The Cultural Revolution intensified Chinese paranoia and introversion, but world events forced new attention on China, a change with great impact on leadership and communication. One immediate cause of this attention was an old border dispute with Russia, whose troop movements caused the Chinese to prepare for invasion. And, though a majority of the United Nations recognized the People's Republic as the only government of China (excluding the Nationalist Republic of China), the United States did not and was thus considered extremely hostile. The Russian threat seemed the most urgent. A clash between regiment-sized forces along the Ussuri River in March 1969 made war seem inevitable.

Together, the Cultural Revolution and the perceived military threat destroyed the old Party structure and greatly increased military influence. Forty percent of the Ninth Congress of the Chinese Communist Party (April 1969) were from the military. More than 70 percent of the Eighth Central Committee, elected in 1956, had been replaced.

Actually, the Ninth Congress may have marked the height of military power, specifically that of Lin Biao. Lin had been Mao's most important ally in instigating the Cultural Revolution and then in restoring order. No one could have been more fulsome in praising Mao, but he seems to have suspected that the flattery was self-serving.

Lin controlled the media, promoted the Little Red Book of Maoist sayings, controlled the economy, and in fact, controlled the nation — but always in the name of Mao Zedong. The Ninth Congress officially recognized him as vice-chairman of the Party and Mao's successor.

Apparently this unprecedented elevation alarmed Mao. Certainly it represented a roadblock to his wife, Jiang Qing, and her Gang of Four. At any rate, Mao began to rely on Zhou Enlai as a counterbalance. Zhou objected to the extent of Party

purges by the army and proposed rehabilitation through education, even for "bourgeois reactionary academic authorities" and
"capitalist roaders in power" (Hsu 1983, 716).

In March 1970 Mao decided to abolish the role of state
chairman against Lin's wishes. The debate came into the open at
the Second Plenum of the Ninth Central Committee in August
1970. Backed by senior military men, Lin attempted a coup,
which Zhou En-lai later called an attempt to kill Mao (Hsu
1983, 718).

Apparently Mao could not challenge Lin directly but
cleverly discredited his chief supporters and brought the other
commanders in line. Relying on his charismatic presence, over
the next several months Mao neutralized most military power so
that Lin first tried another assassination and then fled toward
the Soviet Union, only to die in a plane crash in Outer Mongolia.

The revelation of Lin's treachery was handled carefully in a
manner that illustrates the Chinese method for communicating
sensitive materials. In Chen village, for instance, Communist
party members were routed out of bed late one night in December 1971 for an emergency meeting at commune headquarters.
The meeting lasted for two days; when they returned, not a
breath of the scandal could be revealed, even to spouses (Chan
et al. 1984, 230–31). In order of importance, groups were called
to the commune to hear the news personally—first non-Party
cadres, then members of the peasants' league, and then other
activists. (The study of Chan et al. is an excellent long-term
study of village life, especially on the role of "sent-down" young
people from Guangzhou. The experiences in Chen village are
representative of all of China.)

Finally the entire village was called together, except for the
"bad elements"—former landlords and other class enemies.
While the local militia stood guard, a message from the Party
Central Committee was read aloud. A thick book of incriminat-
ing documents was handed out, even to the largely illiterate
peasantry, but then collected and kept under guard.

The young activists who had been sent to Chen village from
the cities found Lin Biao's treachery to be the last straw. They
had believed all the other stories of the betrayal of the great

Mao, but if Lin Biao could suddenly be changed from paramount hero to unspeakable villain, perhaps nothing was certain (Chan et al. 1983, 230–31).

The new constitution written by the Central Committee downgraded the Party worker from a self-sufficient, resourceful, and loyal revolutionary to a puppet, continuously echoing Chairman Mao. But one can stretch personal charismatic authority only so far. In fact, localism was still very strong, though carefully dressed in leftist slogans. If language is right, anything is permitted.

The Gang of Four (1973–1976)

Lin Biao's fall left half the top posts in the Party and government vacant. At the Tenth Party Congress in August 1973, radicals supported by Mao and directed by Jiang Qing emerged with at least a majority. A moderate group, headed by a rehabilitated Deng Xiaoping, provided some balance, and Zhou En-lai tried to keep the country on an even keel.

Media control was very important to the Gang of Four. "Many times the Gang of Four sat in the very seats where you are sitting and told us what to broadcast," I was told at the Shanghai television station. Jiang Qing's first official post had been in propaganda.

Zhou was enigmatically attacked by the Cultural Revolution clique shortly after the Tenth Congress in a "Criticize Lin Biao – Criticize Confucius" campaign. Few peasants understood, and the campaign died down in late summer 1974. At the same time, Zhou was hospitalized with terminal cancer (Hsu 1983, 725–27).

A dramatic change in U.S. relations had occurred in 1971, when Secretary of State Henry Kissinger secretly visited Beijing. In October 1971 the United Nations voted to turn the seat held by the Nationalists over to the People's Republic, and in February 1972 President Richard Nixon made his historic visit to China, bridging "16,000 miles and 22 years of hostility" (Hsu 1983, 731–46). These great international events had little impact on the peasantry, such as the people of Chen village, however.

The Gang of Four was busy radicalizing the Party, working against the pragmatic policies of Deng Xiaoping. After spectacular initial successes with improved strains of rice, villagers found that crops were degenerating because no one had continued to develop the breed. Dependent on Japanese chemical fertilizer, they were plagued by erratic supplies. They were forced to build a local plant, but it proved to be inefficient. In a replay of the Great Leap Forward, villagers were told to carry out their own agricultural experiments. Since there was no training and no equipment, most experiments failed, and eventually the villagers refused to continue paying for them.

Centralized economic decisions continued to be irrational and even disastrous. Throughout Guangdong Province (the area near Canton) peasants were forced to plant crops that predictably failed because they were not suited to the climate—in the process badly damaging rice output.

Another national campaign called on peasants to "Learn from Dazhai," a model village whose main output was propaganda. The people of Dazhai were supposed to have created new fields by leveling mountains. At great expense Chen village leveled new land, only to find that they had buried what little topsoil there was. Left bald for months, the land was eventually seeded with trees as it had been before. Later the plan for Dazhai was exposed as a fraud (Chan et al. 1984, 239–40).

Some small Chen factories prospered—a brick factory using local clay and grass, a grain mill, a peanut oil press, a yam processing plant, and small sugar and alcohol refineries—and improved village life. Others, less suited to the resources and managerial ability of the village, lost heavily.

Income, which had doubled from 1964 to 1967, stabilized and then dropped sharply. As measured by a day's pay for the best worker, income dropped from one yuan in 1971 to 0.45 yuan in 1975, a particularly bad year.

Party loyalty dropped accordingly. Repeated campaigns had immunized the peasants. Perhaps more important, by now the children of peasants were growing up and using the advantages of primary or even secondary education to judge the Party with more sophistication. They did not believe that things could ever have been as bad as the old folks said, and some could remember the boom times of the midsixties. Cadres stopped

Tian an men Square Incident—More than 2 million people were reported to have gathered in the main square of Beijing to honor the memory of Premier Zhou En-lai and to denounce the Gang of Four during the Qing Ming festival in the spring of 1976. (The festival honors the dead; it is a time when Chinese "sweep the graves of their ancestors" as a mark of respect similar to the U.S. observation of Memorial Day.)

The Gang of Four (Mao's widow and her clique) attacked Zhou's memory and prohibited black armbands, white flowers, or other signs of mourning. But ordinary people braved the police (380 were arrested) to read and copy memorial

poems and listen to eulogies. Wreaths, flowers, and copies of poems and eulogies covered the square, beginning with the Monument to the People's Heroes, shown here (*China Pictorial* 1:1979, 1–5).

Worker Wang Lishan posted this bitter poem in Tian an men Square, attacking the Gang of Four for their disrespect:

> The devils howl as we pour out our grief,
> We weep but the wolves laugh,
> We spill our blood in memory of the hero,
> Fierce-browed, we unsheathe our swords.

Apparently, this outpouring of sentiment rallied enough support within the Party and the army to destroy the Gang. Arrested, they were tried on television and jailed, probably for life.

83

The Gang of Four—Yao Wenyuan, Zhang Chunqiao, Wang Hongwen, and Jiang Qing (Mao's widow) wanted to perpetuate the chaos of the Cultural Revolution. Arrested in 1976, they were tried on television in 1980. Probably Jiang Qing will be confined for the rest of her life.

Jiang Qing is fifth from the right in the picture showing the defendants' faces. She is the black-haired figure almost in the center of the picture showing the tribunal (*China Pictorial* 1:1981, 14). A minor film actress from Shanghai, she led a private life as Mao's second wife until being placed in charge of "reforming" propaganda and the performing arts. From this vantage point she became a key figure in the excesses of the Cultural Revolution. Her clique attempted to seize supreme power after Mao's death.

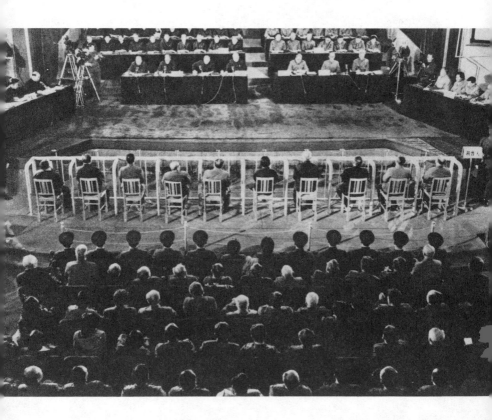

their self-sacrificing and concentrated on enjoying their privileges. Politics became a charade and "looking out for number one" was the order of the day. In 1976 Premier Zhou En-lai, China's most stabilizing leader and her most respected world representative, died.

TIAN AN MEN SQUARE INCIDENT

Attacks on Premier Zhou En-lai and attempts to prevent spontaneous demonstrations in his memory seem to have been the crucial event in bringing about the arrest of the Gang of Four. The demonstrations centered around Tian an men Square, the huge parade and demonstration ground in the center of Beijing, during the Qing Ming festival (a sort of Memorial Day honoring the dead) in 1976. The first wreath in Zhou's honor appeared in front of the Monument to the Peoples' Heroes on March 25. It was followed by others and by a bowl of water and a bowl of earth — Zhou's ashes had been scattered over the fields and rivers of China at his request. The first eulogy was posted on March 30.

By April 4, Tian an men was a sea of mourners, piled high with mountains of wreaths, and flooded by poems and eulogies. It is estimated that roughly 2 million people came to the square that day. But that night the Gang of Four sent 200 trucks to clear away the wreaths, poems, and eulogies. On the evening of April 5, they sent men with clubs and other weapons to break up the crowds, and 380 people were arrested. It is said that it "took three days to wash away the blood spilled that day, but the sacrifice was well made" (Liang and Shapiro 1986, 239). Protests over this desecration of Zhou En-lai's memory solidified the opposition, leading to the overthrow of the Gang of Four (*China Pictorial* 1979, 1:1–5; Hsu 1983, 775–76).

After the Gang of Four (1976–)

Chairman Mao died on September 9, 1976. About one month later, Hua Guofeng was named as his successor, and shortly thereafter Jiang Qing and the Gang of Four were arrested. They seem to have plotted a military coup but failed to win enough support (Hsu 1983, 781–90). News of the arrests apparently circulated by telephone and other private means — the Chinese had closed-circuit radiocasts, restricted publications, and organizational television channels — before any public word was passed. But the news was generally greeted with joy. Liang Heng, a worker striving to become a university student, remembers the day (Liang and Shapiro 1983, 264):

At last we had someone to blame for our miseries. Cadres, workers, soldiers, intellectuals, and peasants, people of all different degrees of political awareness, we were once again swept up in a political movement. All our hate was directed toward four miserable creatures. It rose into delirium. We bought liquor, bottle after bottle until the shops were empty, and paraded on the streets setting off firecrackers until the shells were a crackling red carpet underfoot. The workers in my group organized a banquet. We held it in our workshop, each of us contributing two yuan and carrying in coal burners so we could cook the whole thing right there beside our oily machines. I got drunk that night, drunk so that I couldn't remember who took me home or, in the morning, what had happened to make me feel so incredibly ill.

The media played an important role in legitimatizing the new regime. Other papers followed *The People's Daily* in denouncing the Gang of Four. Among the accusations aimed at them was that they had lied about Mao's last words, the meaning of which would have an impact on the course government would take. The leftists maintained that Mao had said, "Act according to the principles laid down," presumably meaning he favored perpetual revolution. Hua, however, claimed that Mao had written to him, "Act in line with the past principles," and "With you in charge, I am at ease." Millions of copies of this last testament were circulated before the Eleventh Party Congress in a move to strengthen Hua's position. It was a successful strategy.

Once in power, Hua continued to rely on selected bits of Mao's thought for authority. Mao's pamphlet *The Ten Major Relations,* written in 1956, was republished because it rejected extremes and factionalism. Hua also edited the fifth volume of Mao's *Selected Works,* published in April 1977. The book covered works from 1949 to 1957 and presented Mao as a moderate, greatly concerned with economic questions.

Deng Xiaoping was again "rehabilitated," and gradually took over power from Hua. The general tenor of the times was seen in the slogan "Economics in command," as opposed to earlier shouts of "Politics in command." Deng restored the reputations of many of those disgraced unjustly during the Cultural Revolution and improved the lot of workers and peasants.

By 1978 Chen village could see material benefits from Deng's emphasis on economics in command. Political campaigns stopped and compulsory meetings became a rarity. "Bad class" labels were removed after almost thirty years. Teams and brigades were given more freedom to choose their own crops, prices for farm produce were raised, and private production was encouraged. Peasants were repeatedly promised that there would be no more abrupt changes and no more political extortion from higher up (Chan et al. 1984, 261–63).

In 1980 Chen village was for all practical purposes decollectivized. Land was distributed to families by drawing lots, and collectively owned tools were sold to the peasants. Not everyone was happy, for individual responsibility meant some loss of security against drought and other occurrences. But by late 1981 a third of all Chinese farms were under the new system.

Chen village's location was fortunate. It was in a special economic zone and was encouraged to develop Hong Kong trade. Wholesalers from Hong Kong were ready to pay premium prices for vegetables and fresh fish. The central government helped by reducing the mandatory rice tax and dropping quotas on peanuts and sugarcane. Hong Kong's proximity also had other results. Most young people migrated there illegally for easier work and higher pay. As it grew short of labor, the village was allowed to hire migrant workers from other parts of China. In effect, the entire population joined the "bad class landlords," often not even working in the fields themselves.

The village store and even the health clinic were rented out to private entrepreneurs. One entrepreneur used remittances from his children in Hong Kong to go into the trucking business, using a small tractor and a hired hand to drive it. Renting community fish ponds, he hired another laborer to tend them. Finally, he opened a small store. According to Chan et al. (1984, 271–74), he was netting 6,000 yuan annually—three times the earnings of an entire family then working in agriculture and probably thirty times the annual wage in 1975. Scherer (1985, 90) gives the per capita income for rural workers as $122 and for urban workers as $207 for 1984.

Progress is rarely in a straight line, however. Some overly ambitious projects were poorly planned and eventually had to be canceled, with great financial loss to the country (Hsu 1983, 845–46). Freedom of speech that was encouraged in 1976 was throttled back in 1977 when the attacks on Mao and the Party became too pointed.

But generally Deng has stuck to pragmatics to the present time. His approach has been to use capitalistic techniques such as piecework and small private businesses when these prove more efficient than dogmatic socialism. "Practice is the sole criterion of truth," and "Seek truth from facts" became Deng's watchwords—striking at the heart of Maoism (Hsu 1983, 804).

Mao underwent a posthumous demystification, which was summed up in Deng's statement that Mao was "correct in 70 percent and incorrect in 30 percent" — all in all, a kind assessment of the chairman's later years.

Deng's own place in history may well be determined by the success of the Four Modernizations. Originally proposed by Zhou En-lai as early as 1964, they were written into the Party constitution in 1977 and into the state constitution the following year (Hsu 1983, 833). They seek to make China a leading power by the year 2000 through modernizing agriculture, industry, science and technology, and defense.

Deng Xiaoping's revolution

Mao's most devastating legacy was utter chaos within the government. No one could get the most basic information needed to make a government office function — or could not depend on the information if it were provided. Questions could not be decided on their merits, nor could decisions be carried out rationally because of fear and factionalism. Leaders could not expect support and respect from the populace.

The system had been deinstitutionalized, to use Lieberthal's (1984, 20–30) word. Rather than legitimate channels of leadership, the country depended on personal loyalty to one or another of the many factions and on political coercion. Personal influence and corruption substituted for law and reason.

Deng and his colleagues then launched a political reform with six main goals: (1) to cut down on coercion as a "normal" part of politics; (2) to reduce personal patronage, nepotism, and corruption; (3) to strengthen rational, legal processes — though this has involved writing new legal systems, especially for commercial dealings with foreigners; (4) to replace the old cadres (two-thirds of whom had not gone beyond primary school and 9 million of whom were illiterate or nearly so) with well-trained experts in economics, engineering, agriculture, and so on; (5) to rebuild the political structure so that decisions could be made on a rational, pragmatic basis; and (6) to restore the legitimacy of the government and the entire Communist movement.

In reducing coercion, the Chinese have made giant steps in rehabilitating "bad classes." Landlords and capitalists have been renamed peasants and workers, almost 3 million "counterrevolutionary" Party members have been formally restored, and millions have shed crippling political labels. Deng has formally announced that class struggle and political campaigns will not be the driving force of the country's political life (Lieberthal 1984, 20–21). The results are clear from the media. Periodicals, including the general media, often publicize disagreements rather than the dominant Party line.

A striking sign of change has been the enforced retirement of Party and government leaders. Hu Yaobang has said that 70 percent of the leaders in major Party and government departments were to be replaced in 1985. Some 900,000 had retired by April 1985, and he predicted that 2 million of the 22 million Party functionaries would step down by the end of 1986. Similar retirements revitalized the army (Biddulph 1985).

Economic reform was outlined in the May 20, 1985, issue of the *Beijing Review* by noted Chinese economist Huan Xiang. Between 1953 and 1980, he said, the value of China's fixed assets (physical plant, transportation system, factories, and other resources) increased by twenty-six times. Her gross industrial and agricultural output rose by 800 percent and national income by 400 percent, but the actual standard of living only doubled. In other words, more and more capital investment produced smaller and smaller gains.

Deng Xiaoping's answer was the responsibility system. Beginning with agriculture, responsibility for planning and production was turned over to the producers. Peasants were allowed to lease land for fifteen years at a time and even allowed to trade plots, though land could not be bought or sold legally. Key crops were still mandated by the commune, but peasants were given wide latitude and allowed to keep the profits beyond government quotas — an enlightened sharecropping system. The result, according to Huan, was that agricultural output shot up by 52 percent in 1984 alone.

The government intends to withdraw from economic organizations — factories, trading companies, and transportation, for example. Businesspeople will run businesses. Urban enterprises will be given autonomy, and the financial, tax, pricing, and banking systems will be reformed. This will involve several years of experimentation, he cautioned, but China will be open to the world in its search for productive innovations.

"Our policy is to let some people and some regions become rich first," he said. "There cannot and should not be equal pay for all." However, "The government is also taking measures of all kinds to help poor areas gradually become rich" (Huan 1985, 16–19).

Agriculture Ministry officials have said that 140 million rural workers will be moved into business, transport, and service industries in the next fifteen years as farming becomes more efficient. They hope to locate factories and other businesses in the countryside.

Zhang Yi, deputy director of township enterprise management, said that, as of early 1985, China had about 1.7 million rural enterprises with 40 million workers, and that the average urban worker made about $21 a month, twice what farm workers make. All of China's rural enterprises produced $53.5 billion in 1984, he said (*Atlanta Journal-Constitution* 1985a). Some of these enterprises are tabloids, video parlors, and even strip joints, as detailed in chapter 8, and some of them have come under severe attack as sensational and depraved. But they also reflect the relative dearth of media in the countryside. Certainly, increased income, leisure, and literacy will spark media development in the villages.

Many people feared a full-scale reaction when a Spiritual Pollution (*jingshen wuran*) drive was launched in 1983–84. Spiritual Pollution includes advocating Marxist humanism, recognizing alienation in socialist societies, accepting non-Marxist economic theory, and promoting liberal tendencies in the arts. For the media, it includes any discussion of these deviations, plus rock music, vulgar books, pornography, and Western culture in general. The campaign's motives are not clear to China watchers, but the campaign had considerable support. When things began to get out of hand, however, the campaign was quietly shelved. Only a few thousand Party members were expelled and a hundred times as many were rehabilitated (Schell 1984, 182–90).

In 1987 Deng fired Hu Yaobang and a group of university officials, writers, and other intellectuals when student demonstrations threatened to get out of hand. This "Bourgeois Liberalization" movement is discussed more fully in chapter 6.

6 THE CHINESE COMMUNICATION SYSTEM

"Carrying out a revolution is inseparable from two barrels. One is the barrel of a gun and the other, the barrel of a pen. To establish a political power, we must depend on these two barrels" (Lin Biao, cited in Lu 1979/80, 44). "One had to read *The People's Daily* every day in order to know what was safe to say" (an illegal immigrant to Hong Kong from China).

The brief overview in this chapter will outline the Chinese system of communication from two points of view: the sender (the Chinese Communist party) and the receiver (the ordinary Chinese citizen). While the interests of the two are not complete opposites, they are by no means identical.

The Chinese Communist Party and communication

In many ways the Chinese Communist party (CCP) has imitated the Soviet Union, including its system of communication. The main purpose of communication — indeed, of life itself — is to build up the socialist state. That single statement explains much of the difference between Western and Communist theories of the media. News to Communists is not the latest report of an event. It is any information that can be used to build socialism. This dedication was expanded to cover drama, painting, street demonstrations — any verbal, pictorial, or symbolic communication, even what transpires between husband and wife. The Cultural Revolution simply intensified the doctrine of implicit control by the Party.

Mao Zedong often spoke of four tasks for the mass media. The media exist, he said, to propagate the policies of the Party, to educate the masses, to organize the masses, and to mobilize the masses (cited in Lu 1979/80, 45).

For our purposes, however, we need to enlarge Mao's characterization to include several other uses for communication, whether personal or mediated. We need to take into account the role that communication played within the Communist structure itself, to include the roles that it has assumed in more quiet times, and to include nonmedia forms of communication.

One of the first things to understand about the Chinese communication system is that it is primarily a personal, even face-to-face, system. The media have been used as the long-range artillery, to borrow a phrase from Wilbur Schramm. Bombers and artillery can soften up a position, but eventually the infantry has to go in to establish control. In China, the interpersonal network is the infantry.

Even when media resources were available, they were not equal to the task of building a revolution. When the Communists turned to the peasants, print would have been almost useless because of nearly universal illiteracy in the Chinese countryside. The one radio transmitter that the Party had during World War II was of very little use with the masses, since practically no Chinese had receiving sets.

Even today reaching more than a billion people who live in more than a million villages is extremely difficult because of lack of modern equipment and supplies. Newsprint, for example, cannot be imported because available foreign exchange must be used on industry. Since good pulpwood is not grown in China, paper must be made from materials such as bamboo. The resulting grade of newsprint is too poor to hold up on modern presses.

But China does have one resource in abundance — people.

As a result, it has built an enormous personal communication system that can literally reach almost everyone in China within twenty-four hours. The system now includes all the modern media and is growing in efficiency and sophistication. But it will remain a personal system for years to come.

On the other hand, the Chinese people have of necessity built their own network of *Xiao-dao, xiao-xi,* "Little Road News." The people must know what the government wishes them to know. But they must verify such information through personal sources before risking a career or even a life on such "news." The main studies of communication in China are Chu (1978a, 1978b) and Chu and Hsu (1979, 1983). Two works that are still classics are P. L. Liu (1975) and Yu (1964).

Official communication system

What is the CCP's top priority for communication? It depends on time and place. Certainly mobilization was often number one as late as the Cultural Revolution. But today information and economic coordination are far more important. Therefore we begin with information for the masses.

FACTUAL MATERIAL

Coordinating the efforts of a billion people is a most ambitious undertaking. Certainly information must flow nonstop from central planners to production centers and from farms and factories to planners. The masses must be told what is expected, given directions and goals, and continually monitored. Both the personal and media systems are used extensively for these purposes.

Development of the masses is a CCP objective. In addition to political study, the Party promotes broadcasting of classes on various subjects. Books published by the central government, mass organizations, and regional governments place heavy emphasis on education and how-to-do-it materials from art to pig farming.

Mutual international understanding is another very important goal. Though the Chinese are wary of imported ideas, they have taken some surprising steps to let the masses see how China compares to the rest of the world — and not always favorably. Each night a television news feed comes in from the West uncensored, although the only voice is a Chinese announcer. Some movies, television programs, educational and cultural touring groups, books, and magazines are imported. World news coverage has improved drastically since the Gang of Four.

China also has several programs designed to tell the world about the Middle Kingdom, as the people call themselves. In addition to touring Ping-Pong players, acrobats, archaeological treasures, and the like, China maintains worldwide news distribution through its news agency, Xinhua. Radio Beijing broadcasts in many languages via shortwave, and periodicals such as the *Beijing Review* are found in most university libraries around the world. Opening communication links between China and the world was one of the most important and hopeful developments of the seventies.

Another important information objective is providing organizational materials to Party members and other officials, most significantly when a new campaign is launched. For example, policies have varied widely on whether intellectuals should be recruited or purged. When a mass campaign is announced, the cadres must have the current policy explained in detail, with specific operational instructions.

Announcing policy and policy change may come via mass media. One example of signaling a change in policy occurred in 1983. A radio broadcast from Guangzhou was the first official word to the people that sterilization was to be compulsory for at least one of each couple with two children or more (Weiskopf 1983). They were told that urban dwellers who refused could be fined up to 10 percent of their wages; peasants could lose part of their land or be fined.

A particularly important objective of communication is to keep officials aware of what is really happening with the people. Internally, the media act as a sort of inspector-general's office — a quasi-independent auditor or inspector who investigates to see that the glowing reports filed by lower-level officials are true. Information from the media, including widespread complaints from the peasantry and reports of falling production, led the

Central Committee to scale back the commune movement of the early fifties.

Internationally, the regime depends upon information from its diplomatic corps, including Xinhua correspondents, and foreign news agencies. Some material is fed to the mass media. Other stories, including those critical of China, are printed in a restricted publication called *Reference News* available to a select group only. Mao himself approved expanding *Reference News,* which now has a circulation of about 11 million—twice that of *The People's Daily*. Two more layers of classified information media exist to give leaders an unretouched picture of the world.

INSPIRATIONAL MATERIAL

Mass movements do not live on facts alone. There is a general tendency of humans to relate movements and events to themselves, and the Chinese are no exception. One writer characterized China of 1981 as a country in search of heroes. This perhaps has prompted the reluctance to go too far in demythologizing Mao Zedong. In 1983 extensive communication was used to refurbish his messianic stature.

But lesser figures are also important. From time to time the "Learn from Lei Feng" campaign is resurrected. Lei Feng was supposedly a humble soldier, devoted to China and Chairman Mao, who spent his life doing anonymous good deeds. Lei was supposed to have died in a truck accident, and his exemplary life was discovered only through the diary that he conveniently kept. Photographs of Lei caught in the midst of his good turns now grace special museums. Although dramatic, this latest attempt at hero building seems to have created doubters rather than devotees.

ENTERTAINMENT

Life cannot all be olive drab fatigues. But in fervent revolutionary zeal, Jiang Qing, Mao's wife, terrorized the entertainment industry for several years with demands to replace all vestiges of traditional Chinese and Western culture with revolutionary music, plays, films, and operas. And she was notably successful. Since her arrest, artists have considerably more leeway. But, even so, most entertainment today has at least some political content. Opera has been restored, but it is at least slightly bowdlerized. For example, it is not permissible for a stage character to have more than one wife at a time; and a song which used to read, "A man should marry when he is 20," now reads, "when he is 30," to conform with the Party's edicts on delaying marriage.

Entertainment is important to the Party and to the public, as shown by state money spent on touring drama troupes, film teams, recreational magazines, entertainment programs on television, and the one-third of radio time devoted to music.

Personal communication system

OFFICIAL ORGANIZATIONAL CHANNELS

The professional Party and government bureaucracy (these are not identical) extend down to the county level, as did the older forms of government. But the Communist system is unique in using nonprofessionals to reach into every factory, housing block, and farm (9 million cadres were reported to be on duty in 1984) (Scherer 1985, 69). Though the Party tried to institute a professional and ideological bureaucracy even here, the influence of lineage, friendship, and so on, is more important to the people and thus squelched other tactics.

The armed forces. The People's Liberation Army performs an indispensable role in government. Often, during the Cultural Revolution, it *was* the government. It is organized down to the last squad member, and its propaganda apparatus, including propaganda teams, may be used to supplement other efforts. The army was Mao's main source of power after his disputes with Party leaders in 1963. Lin Biao launched the *Sayings of Chairman Mao,* the "Learn from Lei Feng" campaign, and many others through the army. Though he was later purged, his actions probably saved Mao from early retirement.

Mass organizations. Before the Cultural Revolution, there were about 164 mass organizations similar to the Young Pioneers, an organization for young people aged 7 to 14. Eighty percent of those eligible belong (Scherer 1985, 49). Each organization had a national staff and structure and was regularly used for mass campaigns. How were such groups used as communications channels? This may best be seen by looking at the way campaigns take shape.

During the Maoist period, it is said that most campaigns originated with Mao himself, though of course suggestions might come from any of his entourage. Typically, Mao would announce his plan to an appropriate national group—the presidium or a staged meeting. Presumably, he had won over the organizational leadership ahead of time; he was not above stacking the cards or packing the house. Normally, provincial government and Party leaders either helped plan the campaign or were called into a national meeting to plan its execution. Then any national organization involved (and most were) would call a national meeting to explain to provincial leaders just what their role would be.

Often the campaign would have its own special ad hoc leadership organization, which helped prevent forming a self-perpetuating bureaucracy for every problem. Provincial leaders, whether from the Party, government bureaucracy, or mass organizations, would call provincewide meetings to explain goals and set local strategy. Similarly, county leaders would call their cadres into session to plan local strategy.

The mass media may or may not be used to lay the groundwork. When the commune movement was planned, for instance, the media began by reporting successful experiments. But at the beginning of Cultural Revolution, only media under Mao's control were directly involved. These were mainly army publications.

But once the "go" signal has been given, the media are used in two ways: first, to tell the masses what is going on and to inspire, persuade, or coerce them into participating; second, to check on progress by direct investigation and by receiving reports, letters from readers, and other feedback as an indirect report of compliance, success, and needed changes.

Typically, the Communists work through small-group meetings and mass meetings. Ordinarily, the small groups precede the mass meetings, though not always. Small groups bring effective peer pressure on individuals to enforce participation and to root out dissent. They are used to win early converts, as in land reform, or to instruct individuals in their roles.

Then mass meetings are held to give the impression of mass participation, although the general rule is that the larger the meeting the smaller the individual participation. Small groups are then called into session again, perhaps to be sure that new objectives are thoroughly understood or that individuals actually do participate, at least ritually. Finally, there are evaluation meetings at each level.

Reports on participation are rather subjective, but it appears that genuine participation was high immediately after Liberation (the inception of the People's Republic in 1949), generally because of enthusiasm or at least an optimistic outlook on the new regime. This would have lasted until the failures of the Great Leap Forward.

The Great Leap's ignominious collapse demonstrated the fallibility of the regime and the precarious economic situation of the country. It also demoralized middle-level bureaucracy, which took the blame for the failures. This took its toll on the effectiveness of propaganda campaigns.

After Mao regrouped, he launched the Cultural Revolution in 1965. Various explanations try to account for this resurgency of a failed philosophy. It seems safe to say that the rationale was "overcoming" through superior philosophy (a theme running through Chinese thought about the West from the nineteenth century). Mao's philosophy must have been betrayed. Had it not been diverted and distorted by traitors, the argument ran, Maoism would have succeeded. Therefore, what was needed was not new philosophy but new leadership.

This approach fired new youthful fanaticism, starting what became a Chinese Children's Crusade. At this point, the mass media were either taken over by young people or by the People's Liberation Army—in most cases by the army—and mass meetings and small-group meetings were revived with a vengeance. No one dared (at least in the cities and especially in the schools) to drop out of the meetings or to say anything not officially approved. One reason for the constant incantations derived from Chairman Mao was that his slogans at least represented safe opinions.

Mao's death, the overthrow of his successors, and the eventual demise of the Cultural Revolution have had a corresponding effect upon political campaigns, mass meetings, and small-group meetings. Most commentators agree that today these sessions are avoided if possible and slept through if not. Some rank them at the bottom as far as participation and credibility are concerned. Perhaps they will be revived, but for the moment they appear to have outlived their usefulness.

A parallel script could be written for the propaganda troupes, including revolutionary opera companies, movie teams, and propaganda groups from the army, Party, or government. These seem to have been converted to professional groups, in the case of drama and opera, or to be quiescent.

China's latest campaign, the 1983–84 drive to stop "Spiritual Pollution," was canceled in January 1984 because of its political effects. The campaign was directed against unwelcome foreign values, but hard-line Maoists were using it against cultural and economic policy shifts, including increased trade with the West.

Christopher Wren (1984) reported that workers had been called into study sessions, disrupting economic production again, and had been ordered to hand over books, tape recordings, and other "obscene material." The ever-fearful Chinese worried that the new campaign might signal a return to the xenophobia of the Cultural Revolution.

The antipollution campaign's motives are not clear, but one supposition is that it was an attempt by Deng to mollify the Maoists. According to Liang and Shapiro (1984, 159–65), the campaign came dangerously near to running out of control. Leftists tried to expand the campaign beyond political philosophy (including literature and the arts) to social and economic concerns. This, Liang says, shook the peasants' confidence in economic deregulation to the point that some committed suicide for fear of persecution over new wealth. Foreign businesses were also notably reluctant to sign new contracts, fearing that the government was about to be overthrown once more (Bernstein 1985, 42–43; Schell 1984, 182–90).

The campaign even brought out some new Red Guards, searching the cities for Spiritual Pollution. Intellectuals, as usual, bore the brunt, especially those associated with the liberalized cultural policy. Ru Xin, a vice-president of the Academy of Social Sciences, and Zhang Xiaotian, a novelist, published self-criticisms in *The People's Daily*. Zhou Yang, the country's cultural czar, also made a self-criticism, and Wang Rou-sui, deputy editor in chief of *The People's Daily*, was dismissed. Wang's essays, especially "Alienation in a Socialist Society," had been used in a movement to liberate thought. Being alienated from socialism is heretical, indeed.

When it became apparent that the antipollution campaign was interfering with economic and political reform, it was first abolished in the countryside and then quietly shelved for the rest of the country. A few thousand unfortunates seem to have been purged, but at the same time civil rights were restored to hundreds of thousands.

Political participation. The appearance of mass political participation in China is deceptive, for as in most countries, ritual participation (i.e., lip service) is much higher than actual participation. There is some political and economic participation, but wide differences exist between the local and national and the rural and urban varieties.

At the national level, individuals participate only ritually, though Falkenheim (1978, 28) discovered that a lack of political concern was correlated with relatively high levels of attention to media coverage and to ritual support. Interviewing Hong Kong immigrants about their political life in China, Falkenheim found that twenty-four of thirty-seven respondents said, in effect, "If you don't grasp politics, politics will grasp you." In the same vein, failure to participate means that your group leader will make you wear "tight shoes."

Locally, formal participation is much higher. Much depends on your status—are you a peasant or the son of a landlord? How much do you have to lose? Do you have the right to speak based on age and seniority? Are you bucking for promotion, a transfer, the right to go to school? The higher your status, the more you have at stake, the more you want from the system, the more likely it is that you will take part.

More than anything else, popular participation seems to depend on the personality of the unit leader. A confident leader does not feel threatened by complaints and suggestions. An insecure leader threatens everyone under him or her. So the leaders with the best leadership skills have the largest group participation.

Written complaints (rare in Falkenheim's group) were used only if the person was sure of being sustained or if the stakes were high. Suggestion boxes were studiously ignored. Personal complaints, on the other hand, were frequent. Workers try to avoid angering the boss, who controls many rewards such as work points and permission to travel. But retaliation was not considered too dangerous.

One of the group functions is poster making. These posters are generally written only when assigned by an official. They tend to be done by committees and generally echo an official editorial. Little independent opinion is expressed, for no one wants to risk being on the wrong side of another policy shift. The move for "bottom up participation" was taken to mean from the bottom layer of bureaucracy up, not real mass participation.

Participation depends on the question. If the issue is not local, attendance/attention is pro forma except for activists. But thirty of thirty-seven Hong Kong immigrants reported speaking their own mind at least twice a year. Older peasants and workers were deferred to on technical or production issues; political activists, on political issues (Falkenheim 1978).

Even the top layers of the party were shaken up by the next reaction to economic and political change. Beginning with demonstrations by university students over local political procedures, poor living conditions, and a lack of choice in their job assignments, the "Bourgeois Liberalization" movement escalated to include demands for free speech, free press, competitive and democratic elections, and thorough-going reform within the framework of communism.

The beginnings of the movement came to light in the summer of 1986, when both newspapers and scholarly journals began publishing discussions of political and economic thought from Aristotle to Friedrich von Hayek (Gargan, 1987a). Economic reform had been extremely successful; the 17 million self-employed Chinese in 1986 represented a 100-fold increase over eight years. Annual income for peasants tripled between 1978 and 1986 to about $120 per person (Abrams 1986), and urban incomes rose 50 percent to around $300 per capita. These successes emboldened some to think that decentralizing political decisions might be just as profitable.

The Party and government are controlled by a "reform party," centering around Deng Xiaoping's closest aides, including Hu Yaobang and Premier Zhao Ziyang. Their move toward economic and political reform is opposed, or at least slowed down, by a group of conservatives including Peng Zhen, chairman of the Standing Committee of the National People's Congress, and Chen Yun, part of the Politburo's five-man Standing Committee.

Students, encouraged by some university and government leaders, lit the spark on December 5, 1986, with a demonstration at the Chinese University of Science and Technology in the city of Hefei. Their complaint was that Party authorities had chosen candidates for the local People's Congress without consulting the student constituency, an unheard-of demand. Some 1,000 students attended the first demonstration and 3,000 participated in a second protest four days later. "The students' requests were very correct," said Fang Lizhi, a leading astrophysicist and vice-president of the university (Mann 1987).

Fang had already shown signs of dangerous democratic and intellectual bias. Mann reported that in November Fang was quoted by the Shanghai *World Economic Herald* as saying that "Chinese intellectuals should straighten up their bent backs. They should not be completely obedient to the higher level or wait for orders from above when dealing with things" (Mann 1987, 12).

Rallies by "tens of thousands" of students in Shanghai attracted international attention and were followed by protests throughout China. The demonstrators often used classical Western democratic ideas and even appropriated American phrases and symbols such as Patrick Henry's "Give me liberty or give me death," and drawings of the Statue of Liberty (Mann 1987, 12).

The demonstrations were quite different from those of the Democracy Wall movement. Earlier protests were led by much older blue collar workers. These students were only young children during the Cultural Revolution. A pampered elite by Chinese standards, they have been exposed to modern technology as well as to noncommunist thought; their *tatzebao* were often written on computer printout paper instead of old newspapers or cloth (Mann 1987, 12).

The conservative reaction was immediate. Editorials and local Party leaders accused the students of threatening the stability of the country and hinted that they were victims of spies and agitators from Taiwan. The strongest attacks came from *The Beijing Daily,* published by the local Party organization in the capital. Demonstrators were called dangerous cancers and class enemies. By January 6 a front-page editorial in *The People's Daily* signaled the highest level of disapproval. Editorials are approved by senior members of the Central Committee and would necessarily reflect the ruling group (Gargan 1987a, 9).

Several high officials were toppled for their "mistakes" in dealing with students. Hu Yaobang and Zhu Houze, propaganda chief, were the most prominent. Hu Yaobang was general secretary of the Chinese Communist party, leader of the political reform movement, and logical successor to Deng Xiaoping. Two scientists, Lu Jiaxi and Yan Dongsheng, president and vice-president of the Academy of Sciences, were dismissed with Fang Lizhi, apparently because the troubles started with science students.

Limits. For the common people, participation, complaints, and criticism have very clear limits. Locally, a citizen risks bad work assignments, discrimination in housing, loss of work points, and the like at the very least. If the issue really becomes prominent, there is the possibility of purge—or at least of raising a dangerous question or of "bad marks" in one's dossier, which is kept by the Party officials.

Although some questions may be broached at one's own risk, there is no questioning of state interests or policy. One may criticize lower-level cadres, malfeasance, or mismanagement, but open criticism of communism is dangerous. The Cultural Revolution was sometimes seen as a democratizing influence. One could publicly criticize Party members without necessarily being seen as criticizing the Party itself.

One's place of residence seems to make a difference in how one is treated. Many of Falkenheim's informants said that the control system applied only to the cities, not the 800 million rural residents. Rural villages in China tend to be one-clan affairs. Once local administrators are chosen, they can be expected to act in a more humane way than outsiders. As for individual participation, Falkenheim's small sample of thirty-seven included only three who rated their level of political involvement as poor. Twenty-six (70 percent) called themselves nonactivists, and only five (13.5 percent) ranked themselves as high in nonritual participation.

UNOFFICIAL PERSONAL USES OF COMMUNICATION

The Chinese man or woman uses communication for much the same reasons as any other individual. First, they are interested in their own security. Then comes concern about individual economic welfare, relationships with other individuals and groups, and finally amusement, fantasy, escapism, or time filling.

In China's turbulent sea, safety overwhelms other concerns. Chinese history is fraught with war, and the common people have been consistent losers. Even today in the relative calm of the post-Cultural Revolution, waves of "liberalism" are followed by harsh reactionism. Today's hero may be tomorrow's revisionist; it pays to be informed.

At an economic level, communications are tools for routine daily living — weather forecasts, stories that at least indirectly tell of consumer goods availability, notices of entertainment, and so on. Some of the media involved are as simple as wall newspapers posted in the shop or the village center, but they are indispensable.

For many Chinese, the communication system is the main source of educational opportunities. Besides the obvious political education presented through every medium, the would-be scholar may find that lessons by radio or television are the only opportunity for vocational or university-level training. An estimated 600,000 people are enrolled in television courses.

The Chinese use the communication system for social interaction, just as others do. Gossip is a way of life, and the grapevine, official meetings, and mass media all contribute.

Since they live under such difficult conditions — hard work, crowded living quarters, an uncertain future — it is no wonder that Chinese use the communication system for amusement and escapism, perhaps more than most. The Party has always provided models for identification, and now that popular writing for print broadcast and film is back, inevitably Chinese young people use the media to project themselves into a fantasy world.

For example, in 1981 more than fifty different movie magazines were being published in the People's Republic. Romantic novels such as *Love Is Not to Be Forgotten* by Zhang Jie are best-sellers. (Zhang writes of a woman married to a man she does not love. She misses finding true love with another man because both are unable to speak out about their feelings.)

Individuals and groups use the communication system for protest as well. In addition to carrying a grievance up the chain of command in person or enlisting the aid of some powerful friend, the Chinese sometimes dare to air their grievances on wall posters. Some go so far as to print underground magazines to protest against the political system, but they often find themselves in jail. The posting of big character posters was once a constitutional right but then forbidden in 1982. Publication of underground magazines lasted only a few months because of reprisals, including labor reform or even more severe jail sentences.

Less dramatic but far more prevalent is protest through official newspapers or radio stations. Communist journalists claim to use many correspondents from among the workers and peasants. These correspondents are expected to actively report bad conditions, corruption, and inefficiency.

Another channel for protest is the letters to the editors column. Each newspaper or radio station has an editorial staff detailed to answer letters from the readers or listeners. *The People's Daily,* for instance, receives 200 letters a day. Each is read and passed on to the appropriate government office for comment. In theory at least, each letter is dealt with.

INTERPERSONAL NETWORKS

If the Hong Kong immigrant respondents are anywhere near the norm, no one stands alone in China. Everyone has cousins, uncles, brothers—the family binds the country together as it has for centuries. Relatives work to advance each other's causes, whether a transfer to the city or better medical care.

Visiting relatives is an acceptable reason for traveling, and letters and phone calls do not seem to be censored (although only high officials have private telephones).

The Communist party has been responsible for several other networks. Activists in the mass organizations build up a network of friends and acquaintances across the province and even across China. This is particularly true of the ex–Red Guards, comrades in betrayal. These contacts sometimes are international. Communication with Hong Kong and Macao is especially frequent, bringing with it a rose-tinted portrait of capitalism. These contacts, more than any other form of communication, are most influential when emigrants decide to leave China.

Visitors from Hong Kong, especially students, circulate relatively freely. They are welcomed as one might welcome rich uncles, for even the poorest laborer dresses in a Western suit and puts on a lavish feast for relatives, who cannot appreciate the difficulty of accruing even the small amount of money needed. Overseas Chinese also return to visit relatives and ancestral tombs. The local Chinese consider them very naive, but they are able to travel even to remote interior villages, as long as they have relatives in these places. And non-Chinese tourists are no longer a novelty at major tourist sites.

Travel inside China by locals is restricted but not impossible. One now sees vacationing Chinese at popular tourist sites, and it is often possible to arrange a travel visa on "official business" for the commune or factory. Peasants are allowed to become migrant laborers during their own slack season and to maintain small businesses such as food stalls in nearby cities. And accounts of vagrants, people bringing petitions for personal injury, and trials of "criminal elements" indicate that some people travel extensively without papers.

7 TELEVISION, RADIO, AND FILM

The enormous task of reaching a million Chinese villages would have been impossible without radio. Certainly by the time of the Great Leap Forward the Party had realized its electronic potential and had pushed wired radio into most areas of China. But it is television that has captured the imagination of us all.

Television

In spite of high costs, limited programming, and some bureaucratic opposition, television is China's most rapidly growing medium. In 1980 there were around 630,000 sets. By 1985 the number was more than 12 million. Seven of ten families in Beijing reportedly own their own sets. Two-thirds of the immigrants in our study (chap. 2) had watched television, and three-fourths of them used either their own sets or one owned by a friend or relative. Only one in four watched a set owned by his or her work unit.

Nationwide, thirty-eight stations originate programs, with 238 rebroadcasting stations and around 2,000 low-power translators to serve county seats and some rural districts.

The Chinese use a 625-line, 50-hertz broadcasting system inherited from the Russians. However, when color was introduced, they chose the West German PAL system over the French SECAM, which has been adopted by the Russians. By the end of 1980, all stations were reported as broadcasting in color, although not many people own color sets (Howkins 1982, 29).

A black-and-white set costs about $280, or five times the average monthly income, and yet Beijing appliance stores do a brisk business. (If an urban family has three wage earners, the cost is only about seven weeks' wages.) Those fortunates with relatives in Hong Kong have sets brought in. A color set that costs about $500 in Hong Kong will bring $1,000 in China. Smugglers now make regular runs between Hong Kong and the mainland, trading long-buried silver coins dating from before 1949 for electronic goods.

GENERAL PROGRAMMING

What can you see on Chinese television? Most of the country has only one channel, although the larger cities have two, and Shanghai and Beijing opened a third in 1981. The first channel comes from Beijing. Current programming begins at 6:30 in the afternoon with a cartoon or documentary. That is followed by forty-five minutes of news. Domestic news generally comes from one news reader looking unwaveringly into one camera. For variety, films of foreign delegations shaking hands may be shown with accompanying comment. Showcase pieces feature agriculture, factories, trade expositions, and cooperation between the army and the peasants. Absent are all the theatricality and personality of Western television news. But, after all, there is little competition and no Nielsen rating to inspire them.

Foreign news is very interesting, at least to foreigners. It comes in as an unedited general world news feed via satellite from Visnews. (During my stay in 1980–81, I asked why television news was allowed to come in freely, in contrast to print, but got no real answer. The most my hosts would hazard was that Party leaders thought it would be a good thing for the people to see the rest of the world as it is.)

The rest of the evening, at least in the schedule for the first week of June 1985, varies widely. On Sunday, a Chinese dramatic serial is followed by a program of popular science, a Japanese drama, and another ten minutes of news and weather before signoff at 10:35. On Tuesday, however, there are two hours of lectures from 7:30 until 9:25 — mainly a static picture of a blackboard on which a seemingly detached arm writes equations. Some 830,000 students were enrolled during 1984 (Dong 1984, 4–5). This was followed by a television drama, "Truly Great Men."

The second channel is programmed by the city or province where it originates, using a mixture of local programs and some obtained from other local stations. These relatively autonomous groups exchange tapes by mail, since they are not hooked together electronically. Educational programming, operas, poets, and foreign and Chinese films make up the schedule.

In Beijing in 1985 the second channel signed on at 8:30 A.M. and alternated dramas, documentaries, news, and discussions. The third channel came on at 10:15 A.M., with educational programs during the day and entertainment in the evening.

Much of prime-time programming is entertainment. There are some sitcoms reminiscent of U.S. programs in the early 1950s, traditional opera, song and dance fests, and plays especially done for television. Many plays are about the disasters of the Cultural Revolution. These "dramas of the wounded" are not nearly as bloody as the revolution itself but are important acknowledgments of the need to avoid rule by a clique or the "cult of personality," as the Chinese delicately phrase it. Foreign programs such as the BBC series on Charles Darwin are occasionally shown, as well as "The Man from Atlantis," "David Copperfield," "Anna Karenina," and "Madame Curie."

Television was also used to present the live broadcast of the trial of the Gang of Four in the fall of 1980, although some pains had been taken to stage the event. Jiang Qing was allowed her defiance, but the general effect was to castigate the Gang and to warn would-be supporters.

One of the more popular dramatic series in 1985 was Lao She's "Four Generations under One Roof," set during World War II. A synopsis of episodes 13 and 14 was carried in the *China Daily* for June 1, 1985:

Rui Xuan's wife, Yun Mei, has beaten a Japanese child. Da Chibao, head of the prostitution clinic and wife of the traitor Guan Xiaohe, is plotting to capture her and turn her over to the Japanese. But Guan dismisses the idea because Yun Mei's husband is now working for an Englishman.

Gaodi, the Guans' eldest daughter, rejects her parents' plan to marry her off to Li Kongshan, the lecher who helped her parents establish the clinic.

Poet Qian is now reduced to wearing rags and selling paintings on the street.

The Japanese appoint Professor Niu head of the education bureau, but he rejects the offer. He is then bullied and wounded by Chinese defectors to the Japanese side.

After Gaodi refuses to marry Li Kongshan, her younger sister, Zhaodi, volunteers to take her place. Zhaodi spends a night with Li, which annoys her mother, Da Chibao. But her father is pleased with the new arrangements and many of his friends come to offer congratulations about the upcoming marriage. They suggest the Guans ask a Japanese to be the chief witness at the wedding.

Meanwhile, news of Zhaodi's intimacy with Li spreads quickly among the neighbours. People curse the Guans. But Old Qi is rejoicing. His third grandson fell in love with Zhaodi before he joined the resistance forces. Thank God, Qi thinks, his grandson did not marry this immoral woman.

During the night, the Japanese break into Old Qi's house. Rui Xuan, who once refused to work for the Japanese and now works for an Englishman, is arrested.

A certain kinship to American television and classic Chinese novels such as *A Dream of Red Mansions* is clearly present.

All this is in brilliant contrast to the period of the Gang of Four (who practically ran television personally), when only eight model revolutionary operas were shown over a twelve-year reign. (For a good survey of television content, see Chu 1980/81, 34–36).

Central TV in Beijing has released a series of forty-six films shot in various parts of China, including documentaries, operas, and dramas. Documentaries in 1985 included one on China's ethnic minorities, another on "Treasures in the Ancient City," and another called "A Passing Glance at Guangzhou." Sichuan opera was represented by "Stamping the Umbrella." One drama, called "Harbin under the Shadow of Darkness," dealt with the northern city.

Japanese cartoons and drama played regularly in 1985. Language classes taught Chinese, English, and Japanese. Victor Hugo shared the screen with Hansel and Gretel and minicomputers.

Ling (1981, 21–28) frankly calls programs in the early 1980s "artistically immature and nondescript in style." They do, however,

touch on many facets of life—career, friendship, love, marriage and so on. Many are in praise of people and things contributing to the country's modernization drive. Some recall the difficult yesteryears of war or the trauma wrought by the ten years of turmoil [the Cultural Revolution and the Gang of Four]; others deal with bureaucracy, conservatism, special privilege, mentality, social abuses, morality and the legal system. There are also a dozen or so programmes especially designed for children. . . .

The general public in their tens of thousands, however, simply ask for more and better TV shows, in addition to more and better TV entertainments in the form of local operas, songs and dances, musical programmes, as well as cross-talks, ballad-singing and acrobatics.

Ling visited a village not far from Beijing as the television service people made their rounds. She found almost all the families watched "Agent Provocateur," a new Chinese film series about a rich young couple of the 1940s who announce during their wedding ceremony that they intend to join the people's armed forces. They are later victimized by a sham revolutionary. A group of women working at packing quarried stone slabs were busy discussing a documentary called "Believe It or Not." The program featured psychics who could tell what words were written on a slip of paper sealed in an envelope and placed behind their ears or in their armpits.

EDUCATIONAL PROGRAMMING

Central television offers basic courses in science, engineering, and technology. Municipal stations offer courses such as the heat treatment of metal. Shanghai offers medical science by television, and other cities plan their own curriculum according to local needs and capabilities. There are informal exchanges of tapes, however.

The classes are designed for group instruction. Students

must have the permission of their work unit and must be admitted by the television university. Each local group views the lectures in a special classroom and then takes an examination written by the television university to qualify for more advanced instruction. Some find the courses immediately useful for their jobs; others hope to qualify for regular universities.

Workers keep their monthly wages and benefits while studying, even full-time. Their factory pays tuition and laboratory fees and provides other necessary facilities. While on educational leave they live more or less like regular college students, attending television classes together in the morning and studying with tutors in the afternoon (*China Business Review* 1985, 20). Most are highly motivated and study through the evening and into the night. Locally, Beijing television offers lectures for scientists and technicians, advanced courses for primary and middle-school teachers, and basic medical science for junior medical personnel.

More than half of China's counties now have television university programs, which are offered to 20,000 local classes. Eighty percent of those completing courses pass final examinations. In five years the system produced 160,000 graduates — 20 percent of those graduating from regular colleges and universities (Dong 1984, 5).

A nightly thirty-minute English lesson has a larger audience than any television program offered, according to *Beijing Review*. There is no registration or examination, but students are expected to master basic English grammar and about 1,000 words in twenty months. A second series brings the beginner to an intermediate level in about two years. Course guides for the basic program, reprinted more than thirty times, have sold more than 5 million copies, but demand still outstrips supply. The popularity of English (the BBC's English by radio drew 18,000 letters in 1980) led to a new program known as "Sunday English," featuring imported English-language films (Ling 1981).

CONTROL

Normally, ultimate control over broadcasting rests with the Propaganda Committee of the Chinese Communist party's Central Committee. Under the Propaganda Committee is the Ministry of Radio and Television; the central broadcasting services for radio, shortwave, and television; the China Record Company; an acting company and orchestra; the Beijing Broadcasting Institute; and the Research Institute of Journalism. The last two are discussed in chapter 10 under journalism education (Howkins 1982, 26).

The second television channel and local radio is operated by the Party's committee at the province, municipal, or autonomous region level. The broadcasting committees are responsible to local government but are heavily influenced by central authorities. Most counties have a radio station controlled by the Party and the government of the county. These feed the wired radio systems original material as well as rebroadcasts from either of the higher-level programming authorities.

FINANCING

Broadcasting is financed by direct government grants; there are no license fees. Some advertising exists, mainly for foreign consumer goods. Since these goods are typically not available in China to the Chinese, it seems that either the ads are an investment in good will or are directed at Chinese with relatives in Hong Kong. It is not uncommon for mainlanders to specify even the make and model of the tape recorder or television set they want brought in from Hong Kong.

Stations do not have to pay for the right to broadcast Chinese films and of course have no contract problems over residual rights and so forth. Recently, cinemas and live theaters have complained that broadcasting is eating into their box office receipts, prompting stations to develop their own programming.

Radio

If one includes wired radio, the radio system reaches practically every citizen. Radio is China's natural first choice for communication—the Communists opened their first radio station during World War II. Radio is comparatively inexpensive, makes no demands on literacy, and is easily adaptable to various local dialects.

The Chinese have three layers of radio programming. At the center is the Central People's Broadcasting Station (CPBS) in Beijing, transmitting on several frequencies simultaneously. Below that are ninety-seven regional stations with programs on from two to five wavelengths. Then there are 22 million relay stations, of which it is estimated that 1,500 to 2,500 are county stations capable of originating some programming of their own (Howkins 1982, 52–53).

According to the Chinese, approximately 11 people out of every 100 own a radio set, while 95 percent are reached by wired radio. It is not clear if more than one program is carried simultaneously by the wired system, though to judge from Chen village, such is not the case (Chan et al. 1984).

GENERAL PROGRAMMING

The CPBS carries five programs at a time. Two are in Mandarin or *putonghua* for twenty hours daily. A third, aimed at Taiwan for twenty hours each day, is programmed in *putonghua* and the Fujian and Kejia dialects. Minority dialects are featured on the fourth program, and the fifth is directed toward Hong Kong and Guangzhou provinces. These programs are about 33 percent music, 20 percent art and literature, 25 percent features, and 15 percent news (Howkins 1982, 56–57).

Beijing's national and municipal stations transmit three kinds of programming on different frequencies. In addition, the municipal station carries a comprehensive education package covering fields such as Chinese grammar and rhetoric, history, and psychology.

Music has accounted for about one-third of all programming since the central station began FM broadcasting during 1981. The station regularly plays more than 100 songs representing the various stages of the revolutionary movement since the 1920s. In 1985, Channels 1 and 2 in Beijing carried predominantly Chinese music, including programs from Shanghai, a concert by prizewinners in the Beijing children's piano contest, and folk music from the various provinces. In addition, they carried several hours of foreign music, including music from films, Schubert, operatic arias, Mendelssohn, a program by the Voice of Germany, and folk music from Brazil.

Radio carries simulcasts of sports events, which attract millions of listeners. Actual audience research was unknown in China until the first audience study by the Beijing Journalists Association in 1982 (Rogers et al. 1985, 179–208). According to the Beijing study, which is well constructed but difficult to interpret with certainty because of the audience's unfamiliarity with survey research, television viewers preferred drama, followed closely by world news and film. Radio listeners preferred world news, drama, and music and operas. Newspaper readers opted for world news, the activities of their leaders, and sports. (The report categorizes preferences by sex, age, education, occupation, and urban or rural residence. It covers metropolitan Beijing.)

One program, "News and Highlights of Newspapers," claims the largest audience of all mass media in China. This is a CPBS program of news and comments from the country's leading newspapers. It provides an immediate index to changes in policy and insight into the thoughts of the country's leaders.

Regional stations carry material from the CPBS but also originate perhaps twelve hours a day of their own programming, especially in areas where *putonghua* is not readily understood. Ling (1982, 19–23) uses the station at Nanjing, capital of the province of Jiangsu, as an example.

Broadcasts begin at 6:30 A.M. with a national news program relayed from Beijing. Local news follows at 7:00. The "news" is hardly what a Western audience would expect. Some stories include improving the textile industry through a "learn from Shanghai" campaign and ways to improve yields in coastal cotton and wheat fields.

Another series is called "On the New Long March," a reference to the Communist feat of withdrawing to northwest China in the 1930s. The program features scientists, writers, athletes, and others contributing to China's modernization. "The Science Garden" covers a wide range of topics from using satellites for weather forecasting to how to run a washing machine. Infant nutrition, menopause, and the secret lives of jellyfish and eels have been featured. "Across the Province" highlights various locales and events within a featured province. One recent program dealt with Shaoxing, a city inhabited since the New Stone Age. Some stations carry local commentaries, especially since Deng's pragmatic revolution.

The 1.5 million peasants in the Nantong area have wired radio in every home. The radio station there has four editors who coordinate 3,000 part-time correspondents. Among them they produce around 100 articles and a dozen letters every day. From this material is built a forty-minute news and feature program three times a day. The system also carries a three-hour art and literature program and regular five-minute news summaries from national and local media.

A similar service is offered at the county level by the Daxing county network, reaching 500 villages spread over fifty square kilometers about fifteen miles southeast of Beijing. The station has about 5,000 loudspeakers of all sizes in homes and public places, and a staff of twenty-seven.

Since the central radio services can be easily received, the wired network concentrates on local concerns, especially agriculture. In the spring of 1983, for instance, Beijing experts recommended postponing wheat irrigation because soil conditions were already very good. But a county agent pointed out that Daxing had poor soil and had had no rain for several months. The station passed along the information and a bumper wheat crop followed. Local amateur and professional performances are very popular, especially Hebei provincial operas. Another unique service is broadcasting individual messages for fifty cents apiece. Originally, the station was carried on regular telephone lines, but by 1984 it had installed its own network. By 1985 every family was expected to have its own loudspeaker (Xiao 1984, 48–49).

SHORTWAVE RADIO

Radio Beijing, the People's Republic of China overseas broadcasting service, went on the air officially in 1950, aimed mainly at China's neighbors. It broadcast in seven foreign languages. Now it broadcasts in thirty-eight foreign languages and four Chinese dialects to people all over the world. Reception is limited because of a break with Albania, which once relayed

Chinese programs to Europe. According to the *Beijing Review* of May 13, 1985, in one year Radio Beijing received 100,000 letters from 142 countries.

The station broadcasts news, commentaries, regular features, and music. Some features include "China in Construction," a report on national development; "The Third World Marches On," a specialized news and commentary show; "Travel Talk"; "Profiles"; and "Culture in China." The latter carries novels, news of the arts, and interviews with cultural celebrities.

Film

The average Chinese goes to the movies 29 or 30 times a year—double the rate for almost any country and six times the rate for the U.S. Theater attendance is reported to be 70 million per day, 30 billion per year. (For comparison, the average American attends 5.1 films per year, Britons 2.3, and Japanese only 1.4. However, Hong Kong residents average 14.1 trips to the cinema annually.)

Howkins (1982, 75) counted 3,000 cinemas in China, plus 1,500 multipurpose auditoriums and 110,000 film units—90,000 in the countryside and 20,000 in towns. It is said that almost every commune has at least one film unit. The State Statistical Bureau reported a total of 178,000 cinemas and film projection teams in 1984 (*Beijing Review* 1985, 12). Theaters operate with 35 mm or 16 mm equipment, rural units with prints slightly larger than super 8 mm (Howkins 1982, 75).

During good weather, commune movie projection teams come to each village once or twice a week, setting up on an outdoor basketball court or other suitable location. Mosher complained of the poor selection and quality of the movies and equipment. Only a dozen or so films were in the commune library, he said, and so everyone quickly memorized each plot. Just as they do during the traditional Chinese opera performances, the audience spends more time chatting with friends than paying attention to the screens. Also, since the sound tracks are in Mandarin, the operator must stop the film frequently in order to give a synopsis in the local dialect (Mosher 1983, 46–47).

PRODUCTION

Fifteen studios make films for general distribution, but many other units in factories, schools, and communes make an occasional film for their own use. Beijing also has six studios, including one run by the army, and studios specializing in news and documentaries, science and technology, education, and agriculture. The Beijing Film Studios produce general interest fea-

Kublai Khan—One of the most ambitious cinematic coproductions in China's history was the eight-part television movie "Marco Polo." A coproduction by the Italian state broadcasting system RAI, and the China Film Co-production Corporation, it was shot in Italy, Morocco, and China and featured Chinese, Japanese, U.S., and British actors. Ken Marshall of the United States played Marco Polo. Here Ying Ruocheng, a well-known Chinese movie star, plays Kublai Khan, first emperor of the Yuan dynasty (*China Pictorial* 2:1982, 11).

tures. Some provinces, including Guangzhou, Xian, Chengtu, and Inner Mongolia, have their own studios.

But Shanghai has always been the Hollywood of China. The Shanghai Film Studios are the oldest and largest in the country, with nearly 1,800 workers producing more than two dozen features annually. An interesting organizational twist is that five "creative collectives" were recently set up. Each has about 20 or 30 members who work together in planning and making films (Howkins 1982, 71–72).

Since dialog is always dubbed in China, Shanghai also has a Dubbing Film Studio, big enough to dub a feature in five days. In addition, the city has an animated film studio and one for science and education films. An average film is shot in one month on a budget of $80,000. Directors get around $150 a month, though the perquisites such as cars, large apartments, housekeepers, shopping in restricted shops, and so forth, make the job worth much more than it might seem.

China produced 144 feature films in 1983, and a total of 181 new full length films (*Beijing Review* 1985d, 12). In addition, Chinese filmmakers have done several coproductions with other countries. These include "Marco Polo," shown on U.S. television in 1982, "The Marvelous Mongolian," a story of a little horse's journey from Wales to Mongolia, Andre Malraux's "Man's Fate," about a Communist uprising in Shanghai in 1927, and a film autobiography of Dr. Norman Bethune (Mathews and Mathews 1983, 280).

CONTENT

The film industry practically shut down during the Cultural Revolution, dominated by Mao's wife, Jiang Qing. Many of China's best filmmakers were killed, others were reduced to dumb brutes. Nothing but "social realism" of the most extreme propagandistic nature was tolerated. Filming was built around the eight or ten model operas, such as "The East is Red," and "Battle of Tiger Mountain." Now many films expose the mistakes and tragedies of that era. Called "Dramas of the Walking Wounded," they mark an important breakthrough in Chinese cinematography.

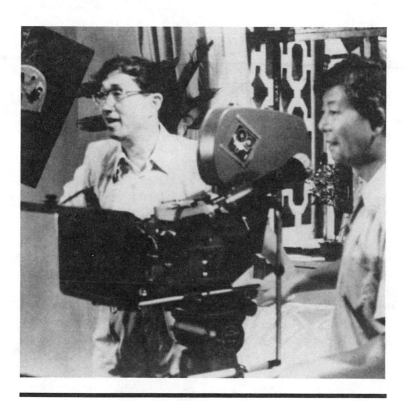

Film Director — Xie Jin works on "The Horse Herder," a 1982 film about the persecutions of an intellectual. Most of his films deal with the tragedies of ordinary people who pursue their ideals despite great personal sacrifice (*China Pictorial* 1:1986, 35–37). Xie represents the intellectual and artistic community, throttled under the Cultural Revolution and the Gang of Four. Those who survived the various purges of "rightist elements" are finding new freedom for expression in China. Though they must work within the basic framework of Chinese communism, writers, artists, and social critics are increasingly able to offer critical comments without which any society will stagnate.

One such film is "Legend of Mount Tianyun," the first film to describe the 1957 struggle between a rightist faction and the Party, just before the Great Leap Forward. The hero, an energetic young man surveying Mount Tianyun, is falsely accused as a rightist and sent to labor reform camp. His fiancée has to break their engagement because he is now a class enemy.

But he never loses faith in the Party and the revolution. Another woman recognizes his worth and eventually marries him. The movie ends on a tragic note, but with a glimmer of hope. The hero is rehabilitated, but his wife dies (*The Asian Messenger* 1981, 6).

Another film, "Maple," portrays the violent factional fighting within the Red Guard. The film portrays the innocence and youthful fanaticism of two middle school students who join different factions of the Guard. Later, driven to frenzied violence, they are killed in senseless internecine fighting. The maple leaf is a symbol of love between the two and the futility of their sacrifice (*The Asian Messenger* Winter 1981, 6).

"Bitter Smile" is the story of a journalist persecuted by corrupt Party cadres during the Cultural Revolution because he will not write lies about a medical professor who has been reduced to cleaning toilets. The film is far from realistic, however, for the labor camp to which the journalist is sent is more like an English country estate.

One of the best and most innovative is "The Small Street," which borrows another technique — letting the audience choose the ending for the film (Wren, 1981). The heroine is a young girl whose mother, dying of cancer, is accused of decadence and fired as a music teacher. The girl has her long hair hacked off by the Red Guard when she tries to sell her violin for food.

Touched, her boyfriend tries to buy her a wig. Since beauty is no part of socialism, he finds that only theatrical performers can buy wigs. He takes one from an outdoor performance, but is caught by the Red Guard when he goes back to pay for the wig. Publicly beaten and humiliated, his eyes are badly damaged. When he gropes his way back to the small street where the girl and her mother lived, he finds the house boarded up and the family gone, a common occurrence when the Red Guard turned people out of home on any suspicion.

As a plot device, the boy is telling his story to a movie

producer. The producer offers three different endings and says, "Let the audience imagine the ending themselves according to their own experience." First, the boy becomes a cabbie and discovers his love smoking, drinking, and dancing in decadent Western-style clubs. "Our generation has become superfluous," she says bitterly.

In the second, the girl is a successful musician. The pair are reunited, and presumably live happily ever after. But audiences prefer the third: the girl becomes a factory worker and meets the boy, his eyesight still dim, as he goes home to see his mother. The girl announces that she has been searching for him as well, and that she will go with him to see his mother.

"Let's shed no more tears," the hero says. "We have withstood it all and we have grown up. We are seeing not the end but a new beginning."

One film, "Unrequited Love," has been held back from distribution because of its ending. It is the story of a Chinese who came back during the Cultural Revolution. Killed by radicals, his final footprints leave a question mark in the snow. The writer, Bai Hua, was severely criticized and has since apologized. Apparently the difference between his movie and "The Small Street" is that the latter allowed for hope (Wren 1981).

Popular films in 1984 included "The Blood is Always Hot," in which a reformer shakes up a silk mill after the Cultural Revolution. He is besieged by the bureaucracy, corruption, and alienated workers. "5 Garden Street" deals with the need to promote young, capable people to important posts (Chen Bo 1985, 8–17).

CONTROL

Filmmakers are ultimately responsible to the Film Bureau of the Minstry of Culture. Economically, they are controlled by the China Film Corporation, which monitors the industry and buys and distributes all films, domestic and foreign. Formerly, scripts had to be cleared in advance, which meant endless delay and a camel kind of script, written by committee. Now a studio can go directly in production — at its own risk, of course.

Until recently, the China Film Corporation bought each acceptable movie at a fixed price, regardless of its length, subject matter, or whether it was in black and white or color. There was some bonus for high box-office receipts, and many special perks for well-known directors and stars. There was no extra fee for TV. The stations simply requested a copy of any new film free. Now a film's price takes into account cost and box-office receipts. Broadcasters have been told that they may not televise a film for at least six months after its release, so as not to hurt the box office (Howkins 1982, 74–75).

8 XINHUA, MAGAZINES, BOOKS, AND ADVERTISING

Newspapers and broadcasting do not make up the whole of the Chinese media system, of course. Millions of copies of magazines and books flooded like a geyser from pent-up authors and publishers after the downfall of the Gang of Four. Advertising is back, and tying the whole system together is the New China News Agency, Xinhua.

Xinhua, the New China News Agency

Xinhua, the official news agency for the People's Republic, celebrated its fiftieth anniversary in 1981. It was first set up in east China's Jiangxi Province as the Red China News Agency. After the Long March, it moved to Yenan, the seat of the Chinese Communist party Central Committee, and in 1937 took the name Xinhua. Operations were primitive. Often correspondents marched all day and then worked most of the night by kerosene lamps. With no electricity available, they had to crank a generator in order to transmit news. In addition, once a fairly permanent base was established, they grew their own food and even spun their own yarn for clothing.

Today, Xinhua, a state-owned and operated agency, has about thirty-five branch offices throughout the country and eighty-two bureaus overseas. It transmits around 50,000 words to the Chinese media every day and about 60,000 words in Chinese, English, French, Spanish, Arabic, and Russian to other countries. The agency has a staff of around 5,000, including 1,000 correspondents in China and 300 overseas. It has exchange agreements with forty-seven foreign wire services for news and photos. Feature articles in four foreign languages are sent out to more than 100 countries regularly. Reporting on the Third World is a specialty (*Beijing Review* 1981, 20–21). Since correspondents mainly hold diplomatic passports, the Chinese will often be found in countries where every other agency has been expelled, as the author found in Nigeria in 1977. They have twenty-eight bureaus in Africa, twenty-one in Asia, and twenty-three in Europe. News from these offices is directed first to a regional desk, where it may be sent directly to clients in the region. Key items go to Beijing first, as caution continues to be the byword for all Chinese journalists. Writing for Xinhua always reflects the official nature of the agency, but foreign correspondents agree that Xinhua now pays more attention to the facts and stresses writing along Western lines.

Xinhua and *The People's Daily* generally provide the most authoritative information and guidance to Chinese journalists and the public. All international news and all important domestic news must be released by Xinhua. Also, Xinhua publishes *Reference News,* the classified publication with twice the circulation of *The People's Daily* (discussed in chap. 9).

Xinhua's correspondents have additional assignments, usually to provide economic and political information for internal guidance. But in Hong Kong the agency has played a special role, that of an unofficial consulate for the People's Republic since 1949. Not recognizing the British occupation of the colony, the People's Republic could not establish a formal diplomatic presence. But the chief of the news agency has always been a political cadre, not a journalist. Xinhua has been among the most important of China's eyes to observe the Crown colony (Schlender 1985, 10).

Finally, in December 1984 the Chinese announced their intention of splitting the Hong Kong agency into two separate offices, a news agency and a political representation. Apparently, the political operation is to take a greater hand in colonial affairs until 1997, when sovereignty reverts to the People's Republic (*Newsweek* 1984).

Xinhua also planned to open a new economic information service in 1985, gathering economic, scientific, and technological data on the area.

Magazines

The number of magazine titles published in China, their circulation figures, and the range of content allowed has been expanding rapidly. In 1979 it was reported that 1,200 legal titles were published. But by 1985 the number of titles was reported at 3,500, almost three times the number issued only six years earlier.

Reported yearly magazine circulation hit a high of 529.34 million in 1958, during the ironically named Great Leap Forward. By 1961, circulation had fallen back to 231.72 million, hitting its low point during the Cultural Revolution with only 22 titles and 27.55 million copies in 1968. By 1975 the trend was definitely up, with 476 titles and 439.28 million copies. Circulation figures are from Chinese postal authorities as reported in *Market,* a newspaper published by *The People's Daily (Asian Messenger* 1981d, 1–4). Today the largest circulation belongs to *Red Flag,* the organ of the Communist party. *Chinese Children's News* sells 7 million copies a year.

Magazine titles range from *Dianying Jishu* on film techniques to *Zonghua Shenjing Jingsheke Zazhi* on neurology and mental health. Each trade or profession has its publication, and general interests such as literature, sports, and photography are not forgotten.

Of the fifty movie magazines currently published in the People's Republic, *Movies for the Masses* is the most popular. Its circulation was allowed by the Party to rise from 4 to 8 million in 1981 to satisfy reader demand, according to Xinhua. The magazine carries news of Chinese and foreign movies; biographies of stars, directors, and script writers; and other popular features. Breaking with tradition, it has also begun to feature attractive starlets on the cover (*Asian Messenger* 1981b, 5). (A letter to the editor of *The People's Daily* concerning magazine covers in general reported that 218 of 792 issues in 1981 featured faces of pretty girls and women. The survey covered 102 different magazine titles. In some categories, especially film and drama, the percentage was much higher. Some 85 percent of film and drama magazines featured women. One even used nude women to compose microscopic patterns, comparing the nudes to "springsprouts" (*Asian Messenger* 1982, 9).

For foreign consumption, the Chinese have six magazines: *China Pictorial, Beijing Review, China Reconstructs, Chinese Literature, People's China* for Japan, and *El Popola Cinio* in Esperanto (Howkins 1982, 87).

CHILDREN'S LITERATURE

China's youngest readers are certainly not neglected. There are forty-six newspapers and eighty-three magazines for children, with a combined circulation in 1985 of 50 million, up by 35 percent over 1983. Fifty of these are news roundups, twenty-seven are scholastic, nineteen are science oriented, and thirteen specialize in the fine arts, music, sports, or recreation. All the editors, reporters, photographers, and artists of *Little Master* are less than twelve years of age. Begun in Shanghai in 1984, the magazine has a press run of 200,000 (*Beijing Review* 1985c, 31).

DISSIDENTS

In 1978 and early 1979, the government tolerated a good deal of dissent, perhaps as part of its campaign against die-hard Maoists. It was during this time that the famous Democracy Wall attracted world attention. The wall was a public space where dissident big character posters were briefly allowed. The attention they attracted from foreigners contributed to their abolition. Schell (1984, 143) reports that Democracy Wall is now plastered with ads, while next door is a private enterprise restaurant serving what was advertised as Western food.

Some twenty or twenty-five unofficial magazines also took

advantage of the brief thaw to publicize dissenting views. *Explorations* was the most radical of these publications.

Sometimes 1,000 copies of this magazine were printed. There were about 200 subscribers at 33 cents per copy. The staff, almost all blue-collar workers or peasants, paid their printer a small salary and split whatever else was left. Most of the money went for paper and postage.

Explorations was best known for an essay entitled "The Fifth Modernization — Democracy." The essay, originally a big-character poster, argued that China could not modernize without democracy. The magazine criticized the state security system and even attacked Deng Xiaoping. Its aim was to explore socialist alternatives for China, but its attempt at intellectual freedom was too much for the authorities to tolerate.

One of its poems by Qu Tian compared Chairman Mao with Emperor Qin Shihuang, a tyrant who unified China in 221 B.C. The editor, Wei Jingsheng, was tried and imprisoned in 1981 on a trumped-up charge of espionage. In discussing the case with Chinese journalists, I asked what guarantees they had for freedom of speech. One editor assured me that Chinese journalists were protected by law and by the Party. Why then, I asked, was Wei in jail?

"Oh," my friend replied, "he was not an official journalist!"

"But that's what freedom of speech is all about," I remonstrated. "If only official journalists are free, then no one is free!"

My friend smiled. "That is an American idea."

Wei Jingsheng was sentenced to fifteen years and was sent to a labor camp. The protests that followed his trial astounded authorities but did not seem to change his fate.

Liu Qing, editor of the unofficial *April Fifth Forum,* took up the cause of Wei Jingsheng. Working out of his own tiny apartment with practically no facilities — not even a telephone — Liu persisted in covering Wei's trial, but, of course, he was not allowed to attend. Liu was arrested two months later after he assumed the responsibility for releasing a trial transcript (Mathews and Mathews 1983, 220).

Later, Richard Bernstein of *Time* and Michael Weisskopf of the *Washington Post* became interested in Liu. Liu's father had worked in the U.S. embassy before 1949 and Liu had graduated from Nanjing University. Assigned to a dull factory job in Shanxi, he was caught up in the democracy movement while visiting a brother in Beijing in 1978.

Bernstein and Weisskopf discovered a manuscript by Liu that had been smuggled out of his labor camp. The manuscript said that he had been kept in solitary confinement in Beijing for five months, under constant "struggle," an extreme critical technique to break down all resistance through incessant psychological pressure with the always implied threat of physical torture or even death. His hair fell out and his eyesight almost completely failed. Nine months after being arrested, he was sentenced to three years at Lotus Flower Temple, which in spite of its poetic name is a labor camp in Shanxi, southwest of Beijing. During the period of which he wrote, he had been working at carrying large rocks and was confined behind high walls and electric barbed wire fences. But still he insisted, "I want to fight until the day I can no longer fight" (Mathews and Mathews 1983, 220–21).

Another unofficial editor-publisher, Xu Wenli, with about twenty others including Liu Qing, produced seventeen issues of their magazine, the *April Fifth Forum,* beginning in November 1978. Xu was a repairman for the Beijing Railway Bureau and was concerned about the public image of his group. Each issue, running fifty to sixty pages, was ceremoniously presented to his shop supervisor so that the group could not be accused of clandestine activities. Several dissidents were arrested in March and April 1979. Xu defended them in his paper, saying that they were no threat to socialism.

But by June 1979 the dissident movement was being put down. Only a few magazines were still publishing, and the wall posters avoided controversial issues. By 1981 unofficial magazines had stopped selling to the public, though some still published free copies for friends.

In April 1981 Xu was arrested and held incommunicado for several months, then sentenced to fourteen years in prison. Even the tame posters still being displayed at the remote site that replaced the Democracy Wall were outlawed when the regime removed a constitutional clause that "guaranteed" the public's right to posters as protest (Mathews and Mathews 1983, 224).

It may be a misnomer to call these and other protestors dissidents. Only a few really dissented from communism — perhaps because such heretics would not have been allowed to speak at all. Mathews and Mathews (1983, 225) tell of seeing a group of ragged peasants on a sit-down protest in front of the Party and government compound in Beijing. Regardless of the true cause, they chanted "Long live the Chinese Communist party. Long live the People's Republic."

Most punishments were handed out without public announcement. Wei Jingsheng was one of the few to be publicly tried. He had dared to criticize Party officials by name and to say that the Party had no business running China, an action severe enough to require that he be made an example.

The Mathewses could not arrive at a count of the active participants in the democracy movement. Xu said he received 100 letters a month, mostly from supporters. He also exchanged materials with unofficial papers in the cities of Baoding and Hefei (not open to foreign travel). There were active groups in Shanghai, and four unofficial editors in Guangzhou tried to organize a national publication in 1980 but were jailed briefly. The Mathewses concluded that activists were probably no more than a few thousand but represented "simmering frustrations felt by millions of educated Chinese."

Actually, most activists were not in intellectual jobs — those people had too much to lose (Mathews and Mathews 1983, 228). Many were former Red Guards, wondering what the Cultural Revolution, or even the socialist revolution, had been all about.

Oddly, although the activists have been silenced, official channels are now more open to criticism. The National People's Congress of 1980 took away constitutional guarantees for wall posters and "great debates." But it was the first congress in two decades to admit foreign observers, and for the first time in memory a few delegates either voted against some of the resolutions or went on record as abstaining. Some delegates to the Chinese People's Political Consultative Conference — an impotent, hand-selected group of well-known Chinese non-Communists — were allowed to oppose resolutions. And the official press is much more open about even unfavorable truths (Mathews and Mathews 1983, 232).

More astonishing has been the growth of semiofficial tabloid newspapers and unofficial libraries, videotape viewing rooms, and booksellers in the mid-1980s. The movement is discussed in chapter 9.

Books

Literature also must "serve the people," and in China, serving the people means serving the Party. During the Cultural Revolution and the terror of the Gang of Four, bookstores were purged of "unwholesome elements," and writers were criticized, "struggled," exiled to "reform through labor" camps, or even killed.

Publishing has grown rapidly since the overthrow of the Gang of Four in 1976—from 2.9 billion copies of 12,842 titles to 4.5 billion copies of an estimated 20,000 titles in 1980. This translates into 4.5 copies of books per person. Only about 4,000 titles were on sale at the height of the Gang's power (Fan 1981, 19–23).

Reading is still a city pastime because of rural illiteracy and long working hours. It is not an easy sport, because library lending is discouraged and too much interest in dangerous topics or writers may bring severe punishment. Popular books are in very short supply, often being sold out the back door by bookstore clerks to their friends. Required texts for educational programs may be so scarce as to be rationed, and seats in the university libraries can be had only by standing in line. Many library attendants resent the few privileges given students; as a result, checking out a book becomes an exercise in patience or futility.

The main library in Shanghai is jammed with users. My examination of the card catalog for works in areas such as economics or mass communication revealed little except very old works, generally of an elementary nature. There was nothing on the effects of mass media, for example, except the sayings of Chairman Mao.

Literary Master — Ba Jin has been called the master of Chinese literature in the present era. Persecuted by the Gang of Four, he began a new book, *Reflections,* at the age of 81 (*China Pictorial* 1:1980, 14). Though the life of a Chinese intellectual is uncertain at best, authors, journalists, actors, teachers, and others are offering their critique of Chinese society in hopes of correcting mistakes and improving the future.

PUBLISHERS AND PUBLISHING

Still, tomorrow seems brighter. More than fourteen times as many books were printed in 1979 as in 1950, and writers and publishers are becoming more daring. "Breaking through the taboos of the Gang is far from enough," Wei Junxuan, vice-director of the People's Literature Publishing House, has said. "We need to free ourselves from straitjacket thinking. We had debates over almost every book before publication, but it turns out that those over which we had the biggest debates are the ones readers like best" (Fan 1981, 19).

There are about 200 publishing houses in China, of four main types. Reporting directly to the National Publishing Administration are thirteen publishers, including the People's Publishing House, specializing in socialist economics; the People's Literature Publishing House; and the People's Art Publishing House.

About eighty publishers are run by government departments or mass organizations. These include the People's Communications Publishing House, People's Medical Publishing House, Nationalities Publishing Company for ethnic works, Workers' Press of the All-China Federation of Trade Unions, and Physical Culture Publishing House.

Ninety publishers belong to provinces, municipalities, and autonomous regions. These used to be limited to regional interests, but the enormous backlog of manuscripts has turned some into national distributors. The Sichuan house has published more than 500 books by well-known writers for national distribution. Shandong, Jilin, Hunan, Zhejiang, and Jiangsu provinces are gradually becoming national publishing forces (Fan 1981, 22).

The eighty-year-old Commercial Press concentrates on reference books and Chinese translations of foreign works on social science. The sixty-year-old Chung Hua Book Company is interested in classics in philosophy, literature, and history. Sanlian Publishing is a combination of three houses that published "progressive" works from the 1930s on. Suspended for ten years during the Cultural Revolution, it has recently published translations of foreign books on China such as Edgar Snow's *Red Star over China,* Lois Wheeler Snow's *Death with Dignity,* and Anna Wang's *I Fought for Mao.*

The People's Literature Publishing House sponsors classics such as *A Dream of Red Mansions, Water Margin,* and *Romance of the Three Kingdoms.* Especially well known is *Red Mansions,* an eighteenth-century soap opera on the corruption, decay, and destruction of a rich family. It could well find its place on American daytime television with a little rewriting. One reason for its repeated publication is its condemnation of feudalism. Probably the reason for its popularity is its folk art quality. Another such classic is Lu Hsun's short book, *The True Story of Ah Q.* Lu (1881–1936) is called the "chief commander of China's modern cultural revolution." Using "literature as a weapon of struggle," he began in 1918 to publish a series of stories attacking China's feudal society.

Ah Q is the story of a feebleminded laborer who is accused of robbing a rich family and executed, mainly because he was the most convenient suspect. He serves as an example of the cruelty of feudal society (Lu 1977, 64–67):

Ah Q was lifted on to an uncovered cart, and several men in short jackets sat down with him. The cart started off at once. In front were a number of soldiers and militiamen shouldering foreign rifles, and on both sides were crowds of gaping spectators, while what was behind Ah Q could not see. Suddenly it occurred to him — "Can I be going to have my head cut off?" Panic seized him and everything turned dark before his eyes, while there was a humming in his ears as if he had fainted. But he did not really faint. Although he felt frightened some of the time, the rest of the time he was quite calm. It seemed to him that in this world probably it was the fate of everybody at some time to have his head cut off.

He still recognized the road and felt rather surprised: why were they not going to the execution ground? He did not know that he was being paraded round the streets as a public example. But if he had known, it would have been the same; he would only have thought that in this world probably it was the fate of everybody at some time to be made a public example of. . . .

As for any discussion of the event, no question was raised in Wei-chung. Naturally all agreed that Ah Q had been a bad man, the proof being that he had been shot; for if he had not been bad, how could he have been shot? But the consensus of opinion in town was unfavourable. Most people were dissatisfied, because a shooting was not such a fine spectacle as a decapitation; and what a ridiculous culprit he had been, too, to pass through so many streets without singing a single line from an opera. They had followed him for nothing.

The Communists continue to publish *Ah Q* as a condemnation of preliberation China. However, a certain similarity between Ah Q's ordeal and the Communist show trials must have struck a few readers.

Ninety contemporary works were published in translation in 1980. They included Herman Wouk's *The Winds of War,* which sold 400,000 copies, Irwin Shaw's *Rich Man, Poor Man,* Graham Greene's *The Heart of the Matter,* and a collection of short stories by Isaac Bashevis Singer. Under way are three works, one surveying contemporary foreign literature, one on foreign classics of art and literature, and a third on literary backgrounds (Fan 1981, 22).

China's 500 million youth make up the biggest reading market and are served by the China Youth Publishing House and the China Children's Publishing House. *Love, Marriage and Family* and *Ideals, Sentiment and Spiritual Life* sold a million copies for Youth Publishing.

Selling a million copies of a reference book is a matter of course. The *Xinhua Dictionary* for primary and middle-school students has sold 80 million. Textbooks for English lessons by television have sold 5 million. *Sexual Knowledge* and *Essentials for Newlyweds* cannot be kept in stock.

Chinese publishers are also cooperating in joint publication with other countries. In the United States, the Science Publishing House and the Popular Science Press, in conjunction with Time-Life Books, are producing in Chinese the *Life Nature Library, Life Science Library,* and *Children's Treasury of Scientific Knowledge.* China Art Publishing and the Kodansha Publishing House of Japan are producing a set of travel guides, and the Yugoslavs are collaborating on a pair of art books.

In addition to the official publishers, unofficial or semiofficial publishing ventures abound, according to Mathews and Mathews (1983, 296). Newspapers regularly denounce the use of government presses, mimeographs, and papers for unauthorized (but profitable) publishing. One government office was said to be publishing Western detective stories. In Hubei Province, a city residents' committee issued opera librettos. In 1984–85 tabloid newspapers sprang up like mushrooms. Other offices printed mathematical games books, which are very useful for fortune-telling. Naturally, since such ventures are clandestine, there is no tax on them. Official publishing houses and bookstores are supposed to make a profit, which is then taxed away by the government.

Books are sold by the Xinhua Shudian, the New China Bookstore, which has 5,000 branches throughout China. The organization is responsible for the distribution of all books produced by national publishers and for coordinating sales of regional productions. Foreign-language books are handled sepa-

Twenty-two Years of Exile — Ding Ling, the most famous woman writer among early Chinese communists, was in jail or exiled to the countryside from 1957 until 1975 (*China Pictorial* 10:1980, 19). Her first brush with authority came over a mild article suggesting that the revolution ought to treat women more as equals. Her most famous book, *The Sun Shines over the Sangkan River,* won the Stalin Prize for Literature in 1951 in spite of its implicit criticism of greed shown by some cadres. As of 1987 she is said to be working on a sequel.

rately by Waiwen Shudian, the Foreign Languages Bookstore, with sales outlets in all major cities. Many of the bookstores operate reading rooms, including some specializing in comics for youngsters (Howkins 1982, 91).

WRITERS

Liu Bingyan, who writes for *The People's Daily,* is considered the most provocative writer today by Chinese intellectuals. He often deals with bureaucratic bungling, a topic about which the Chinese know a great deal. Using discretion about which bureaucrats to attack, Liu remains fairly safe (Mathews and Mathews 1983, 295).

Ding Ling, perhaps the most famous woman writer among Chinese Communists, disappeared for twenty-two years after being denounced in the first antirightist campaign of 1957. Ding was no stranger to political persecution. She first drew Mao's wrath in 1942 with an article on International Women's Day that mildly criticized male Communist leaders because of the repression of women in Yenan. She was sentenced to thought reform for daring to suggest that there were flaws in paradise.

Uncowed by the experience, Ding wrote about land reform in the district to which she had been exiled. *The Sun Shines over the Sangkan River* won the Stalin Prize for Literature in 1951, and many feel that it is still one of the best pieces of literature from Communist China. Her intention was to propagate the Party line about land reform, but as a good writer she let her characters speak as they really do. A landlord says, "The Communists always say they are working for the poor. . . . But that is just so much fine talk. . . . In Kalgan who lives in the best houses? Who rides in cars? Who are always coming in and out of fine restaurants? Aren't they the ones who have grown fat?"

Continued efforts to persuade young intellectuals to write the truth led to her censure in 1955 and exile in 1957. After four months of attempted brainwashing, she was banished to a small village near the Russian frontier. Later she was attacked by the Red Guard. From 1971 to 1975 she was placed in solitary confinement in a "cow shed," a term for a jail for political prisoners.

Released from jail in 1975, she was sent to another farm,

this one in a remote area of central China. In spite of intense pain and continued danger, she resumed writing. She still emphasizes "telling the truth" and says that villagers spoke openly with her because of her status as a prisoner. "When there are only two persons, they tell the truth," she told *News Front,* a magazine published by *The People's Daily.* "When there are three, they tell jokes; and when there are four, they speak falsehoods."

In spite of everything, Ding Ling remains optimistic, at least according to official accounts. She is said to be working on a new novel, *In the Cold Days,* a sequel to *The Sun Shines over the Sangkan River* (Wei 1984, 36–39).

Novels from the Cultural Revolution are quite popular. Chen Dengke, jailed by the Gang of Four, has written *Breaking New Ground.* The sufferings of three air force generals are told in *Song of the Generals* by Mo Yingfeng, and *A Woman Prisoner's Account* is by Tan Lin, a young worker.

By and large, novelists stay within bounds, partly from fear and partly as a reflection of Chinese philosophy. Zhang Xianling has written a series of novels describing his persecution, beginning with the antirightist movement of 1957. But he displays no condemnation, resentment, or indignation. Instead, in the preface to the English edition of *Mimosa* he writes: "In a country with such a long history and in such a backward state of economic development, modern political trends may superficially appear to be determined by particular people. In fact, they are governed by a variety of factors answerable to historical categories and not to individual will" (Zhang 1988, 81).

Women are becoming an important literary force in China. Several who survived World War II, revolution, rectification, and the Cultural Revolution are in their eighties, but the main feminine writers, in their forties, were educated before the Cultural Revolution. They include Zhang Jie, Chen Rong, Li Huixin, Wen Xiaoyu, Ling Li, Dai Qing, and Dai Houying.

Zhang Jie is well known for *Love Must Not Be Forgotten.* A young woman discovers letters between her late mother and the man she truly loved, although, out of a sense of duty, her lover married the widow of a man who died to save him. It struck a sympathetic chord at the time Chinese young people were rejecting arranged marriages. Her later *Heavy Wings* is considered a better work, dealing with broader problems of confrontation between progressives and conservatives in industrial reform (Liang and Shapiro 1984, 91).

Chen Rong created a sensation with "At Middle Age," dealing with problems of middle-aged intellectuals in China. Ling Li, who began to study history when she was blocked from becoming an engineer by the Cultural Revolution, has written a novel, *Star Grass,* about a Qing dynasty uprising by peasants.

The youngest group of prominent female writers grew up during the Cultural Revolution. Many were sent to the countryside for several years under the Gang of Four. They are not so sure about the inevitability of history. Zhang Kangkang, for instance, focuses on the conflict between the morality of the young and their elders in "Going Far Away" and "Summer." Wang Anyi finds beauty in ordinary people in stories such as "The Train Arrives at the Last Stop" and "Mediocre People" (Wei 1984, 36–39).

Advertising

Until the Cultural Revolution, the Chinese used advertising — including ads in newspapers, in telephone directories, at movies, at point of sale, and on billboards. No ads were allowed on radio or television, except for political bombardment. The main mass medium for advertising was the newspaper. *Ta Kung Bao* and *The Worker's Daily* carried most national ads, although *The People's Daily* also carried some. Major metropolitan papers carried ads for consumer and industrial goods and services, including book and movie ads, radio programs, sports and cultural events, wedding announcements, and paid obituaries. J. Chu (1982, 56) reports many ads looking for lost family members.

Between 1966 and 1978, advertising completely disappeared on ideological grounds, even window displays. But with the downfall of the Gang of Four, advertising's usefulness in directing and channeling demand was recognized once more. Even television was opened to foreign advertising, though under strict supervision (J. Chu 1982, 40–45).

In the sense of attracting public attention, advertising never left China. The posters of Mao, Stalin, and Lenin; the interminable sloganeering; and the wall posters were certainly advertising. But capitalistic advertising (that is, for products) returned to China after ten years' absence in 1979. According to Radio Beijing, commercials were first broadcast on Shanghai radio beginning with the Chinese New Year in January 1979. At the same time, magazine, newspaper, and movie ads reappeared and billboards and shop-window displays were restored.

The first spot for "Happiness Cola" was shown on Shanghai television on March 11, 1979, followed by ads on the Guangdong Province station. Domestic and foreign goods ranging from light bulbs and cold cures to Swiss watches and color television sets were featured. Most seemed to be aimed at the Chinese who have remittances from outside the country or visitors from Hong Kong or overseas who can bring gifts or cash. L. Chu (1979/80, 56) wrote:

People in Hong Kong and elsewhere have been flooded with letters from their relatives asking for specific brands of TV sets, cassette radios or watches. Some of the brands are even unknown to the letter receivers. At Shumchun, the Chinese town bordering Hong Kong, people carrying TV sets on bamboo poles have become a common sight for the past year.

Apparently, advertising from foreign corporations is carried mainly because it produces revenue; products are not necessarily available. Domestic ads are considered a guide for consumers and a necessity for the improvement of Chinese goods. Advertising seems to be thought of as a part of the drive to test truth by results, allowing local enterprises much greater leeway in planning and marketing. Rather than trying to regulate all production through central planning, the Chinese have adopted some aspects of regulation by the market—that is, efficient producers will be rewarded, although nothing much seems to happen to inefficient producers.

Domestic advertising has saved several factories, according to *The People's Daily*. In a comment that might well have come from a U.S. publisher, the newspaper boasted that orders came like "avalanches" after a Hunan thermal materials factory began advertising in the *Daily*. However, Chang Kuo-sin reports that there were many ads on television in late 1984 for goods that were not available in the stores. They could be ordered from the Chinese factories where they were supposedly being manufactured, but orders were never filled (Chang 1985a).

Several ad agencies have been formed inside China, and agents have been appointed in Hong Kong and abroad. Actual ad revenues were reported to be $120 million for 1984 (Scherer 1985, 90). One disadvantage for ad agencies is that no audited reports of circulation are available. Some of the drearier publications in which ads appear go unsold at any price, while others with a very high pass-along rate are read by several times the stated circulation figure.

Media available for advertising range from video cassettes, which the Chinese will display in Beijing or take to the appropriate ministry or factory, to advertising at sponsored sports events such as the tennis match between Bjorn Borg and John Alexander in 1979. There are even television ads on the express train from Guangzhou to Hong Kong (Howkins 1982, 109–11).

9 NEWSPAPERS

Communist "newspapers" are not "news" papers in a Western sense but house organs for the Party/government. Lu (1979/80, 44–52) put it this way:

From the very beginning, the Chinese Communist press has been learning from the Russians. It is neither the traditional intellectual endeavor, nor the western free enterprise, but an organ of proletarian dictatorship. Its propaganda functions, as prescribed by the Party, are to carry out the Party's intentions and to look upon the materialization of Communism as its highest goal. During the present stage, it must struggle for the materialization of socialism and the consolidation of proletarian dictatorship.

Newspaper circulation

Newspaper exposure is conventionally measured in terms of copies sold. The Chinese daily press has a run of more than 116 million copies, or 11.6 for each 100 people. Comparatively, this is a very low figure. Japan and Sweden print more than 50 copies per 100. The United States produces 30 copies per 100,

Thailand 24, the USSR 10, Nigeria 7, and Pakistan 6. (The Chinese may have more readers per copy, but no evidence is available.)

China has 1,300 newspapers of all types, according to the *Beijing Review* in 1985. Thirty-six are national; the rest are provincial or municipal, with a few district and county papers. Major national papers are *Renmin Ribao (The People's Daily), Gongren Ribao (The Workers Daily), Jiefangjun Bao (The Liberation Army Daily), Guangming Ribao (The Brightness Daily,* which caters to intellectuals), *Zhongguo Nongmin Bao (The Chinese Peasant's Paper), Zhongguo Qingnian Bao (The Chinese Youth News),* and *Zhongguo Shaonian Bao (Chinese Children's Paper)* (Zhou 1981, 23).

The largest and most important paper for the general public is *The People's Daily,* which distributes around 5.3 million copies daily. The paper is printed in Beijing and twenty other cities in China plus Hong Kong and Tokyo. The pages are transmitted to ten printing sites by radio facsimile and to the others by matrixes of entire pages sent by air.

Secret publications

Beyond the open media lie four levels of *neibu* — "internal" or restricted publications (see Butterfield 1982, 388–91). Level one of classified news is *Reference News,* or *Cankao Xiaoxi.* Its circulation has been variously given as 8.47 million, 10 million, and 11 million. *Reference News,* a four-page tabloid, reprints foreign articles on international affairs, including some criticisms of China and communism. Some dispatches by foreign correspondents on Chinese domestic affairs are also carried. Butterfield (1982, 390) says that any Chinese can subscribe to *Reference News* for 50 cents a month. Mathews and Mathews (1983, 173) say that one must be a regular member of some factory, university, or office unit, and that the price is about 30 cents a month. It is not generally available to foreigners (Zhou 1981, 24).

This publication and other classified materials serve many

important functions, as Mathews and Mathews (1983, 173–75) pointed out:

> Some of our Chinese friends were so stunned when the officials occasionally reported real facts about events like the Peking railroad station bombing that they tended to disbelieve them. Their local newspapers were little better, usually reprinting articles from *The People's Daily,* although some publications, such as the *Peking Evening News,* provided some crime stories and other light features that readers found refreshing diversions.
>
> For facts, the Chinese turned by the millions to *Cankao Xiaoxi,* a small tabloid that is unique in the world. Translated, it is called *Reference News,* a latter-day version of the emperor's *Peking Gazette.* . . .
>
> They printed items so controversial they could never be comfortably raised in the official press, like a *Los Angeles Times* editorial questioning the need to sell U.S. arms to China and a wire-service account of the Dalai Lama asking for more freedom for Tibetans. The newspaper published reports by foreign correspondents, or pro-Communist Hong Kong papers, explaining what was happening in China—such as challenges to Deng Xiaoping's group—with a clarity and speculative boldness that was too much for the masters of obliqueness in the official Chinese press. This way the message got to the people without anyone being blamed for revealing too much. It seemed clear to us, after talking to some Hong Kong editors, that Chinese officials sometimes even intentionally leaked news to them so that it could be printed in *Reference News.* One night on Anhui's Yellow Mountain a Chinese journalist, after a few beers, gave Jay a little speech: "Sometimes there are things we have difficulty criticizing or even noticing in our country. We rely on you foreigners to write about them. This gets attention. Your pieces appear in *Reference News!* And that helps us."

Atwood and Lin (1982, 240–48) were able to analyze eleven issues of *Reference News* from 1979. The average issue carried twenty stories. About 48 percent were hard news, 23 percent were commentary, and 29 percent were features. Some 73 percent of the stories were on three topics: foreign relations (86 stories, 38.7 percent), economics (47 stories, 21.2 percent), and domestic politics (29 stories, 13.1 percent). The subject of refugees from Indochina accounted for 26 stories, or 30.2 percent, of the articles on foreign relations. Energy problems took up 17 articles or more than 33 percent of the economics stories.

Hard-news stories about non–Third World countries were

reprinted about 4.8 days after their original publication. Features about the same countries took the longest time to get into print, about thirty-one days. In general, hard news was reported in four to six days, commentaries within seven or eight days, and features in fourteen to twenty days.

More than half the stories came from the four Western agencies (Associated Press, United Press International, Reuters, and Agence France-Presse). The AP and UPI were credited with 82 items, and all U.S. sources accounted for 106 citations. Japanese sources provided 10.6 percent, and another 12 percent came from West European newspapers and magazines. TASS accounted for only 1.6 percent. The United States received the most coverage, followed by China and the Soviet Union.

Two-thirds of the forty stories about China were on her domestic politics and economics. All the lead stories were related to national development, specifically the Four Modernizations. Only two items were unfavorable—a feature on the inadequacies of Chinese tourist hotels and a Japanese interview with Nationalist president of China (Taiwan) Chiang Ching-kuo in which he declared the Republic had been fighting for freedom and against communism.

News about India, Indonesia, and the Soviet Union remained negative between 1960 and 1979. Coverage of Taiwan shifted from negative to neutral, while the United States changed from a weakening warmonger to a friendly country assisting the People's Republic in achieving the Four Modernizations. Mao (1965, 369–70) explained:

We have now decided to increase the circulation of *News for Reference* from 2,000 to 400,000 so that it can be read by people both inside and outside the Party. This is a case of a Communist Party publishing a newspaper for imperialism, as it even carries reactionary statements vilifying us. Why should we do this? The purpose is to put poisonous weeds and what is non-Marxist and anti-Marxist before our comrades, before the masses and the democratic personages, so that they can be tempered. Don't seal these things up, otherwise it would be dangerous. In this respect our approach is different from that of the Soviet Union. Why is this vaccination necessary? A virus is artificially introduced into a man's body to wage "germ warfare" against him in order to bring about immunity.

Atwood and Lin could not determine how much editing

had been done on the issues of *Reference News* they studied. In a few instances, they were able to determine that the translation was faithful to the original, except for paragraphs cut from the end (a standard editing practice).

Page one of each of the eleven consecutive issues analyzed carried commentary about the People's Republic, with emphasis on development. Page two carried international news, especially on the major powers, including political analysis and economic reports. Page three was also international but focused on the Third World. Page four reprinted science, sports, and features.

Publications similar to *Reference News* are published in the USSR. *Atlas* carries translations of Western news for "mass propagandists." *White TASS,* apparently named for the fact that it is printed on white paper rather than the ordinary green or blue paper, is more restricted in circulation but provides more depth of material (Kaiser 1976, 252–53; Smith 1976, 474–75).

The second level of Chinese classified news is *Reference Material,* or *Cankao Ziliao,* a more detailed digest of foreign news articles. Printed twice a day, it averages 100 magazine-sized pages in the morning and 50 in the afternoon. In large characters for easy reading by elderly officials, it is available only to Party members and cadres from section chiefs upward through their Party organizations, not to individuals (Butterfield 1982, 390; Mathews and Mathews 1983, 176; Lu 1979/80, 47).

Reference Material is almost certainly issued by Xinhua, since no other organization has a large enough staff for the job. It often carries full translations of even lengthy reports within two or three days. The effort involved may be seen in Rudolph's estimate that an English translation of each day's work would be 300 to 400 typed pages long.

Next are publications known as *nei-can* (internal reference), which are distributed only to officials equivalent in rank to deputy cabinet ministers. Each ministry puts out its own, supposedly unretouched status report on its area of responsibility. These circulate to other ministries.

Most widely read of the *nei-can* are those published by *The People's Daily* and Xinhua, the news agency. *The People's Daily* boasts a very large staff, a reported 630 journalists for this eight-page paper. Its policy is to allow them to work on *nei-can* entitled *Brief Reports on The People's Daily Work Conditions* and *Life in the Editorial Department.* *Brief Reports* carries stories on problems not suitable for publication elsewhere or whose publication is yet to be decided. Minor problems are published in *Life.* *People's Daily* reporters can investigate very sensitive problems such as official corruption, strikes, ethnic friction, and discrimination against women (Butterfield 1982, 391; Lu 1979/ 80, 48). Xinhua publishes *Trends of Journalistic Work.* It frequently reports the opinions of provincial and municipal Party committees on touchy problems (Lu 1979/80, 48).

At the top of the secrecy ladder is a special digest called *Cable News,* which is meant only for the Central Committee and top military commanders. It carries major news flashes from China and the world (Butterfield 1982, 391).

Open publications

At the local level, each of the twenty-nine provinces and municipalities has a daily newspaper of its own. Most provincial newspapers are published in and named for the provincial capital; for instance, the *Guangming Ribao* is published for Guangdong Province. In large cities such as Shanghai, several papers flourish. Shanghai has its *Liberation Daily* and *Wen Hui Bao,* plus some tabloids such as *Youth News.* Guangzhou has a popular evening paper called the *Ram City News.*

A few provinces also publish a farmer's paper such as the *Yunnan Farmer's Daily,* which is published in Kunming. Where there are ethnic minorities, papers are published for them. In Hungtai and Chinpo Autonomous Chow on the Laos-Burma border there is the *Unity News* for the Thai people who live there (Lu 1979/80, 46–47). In 1983, the Chinese reported seventy-two local newspapers with an average annual circulation of 96.113 million (Scherer 1985, 315).

There are also national special-interest papers including sports, health, law, music, and economics. The *World Economic Herald* in Shanghai is a digest of world economic news that began publication in 1979 and eleven months later was near its break-even point of 250,000 circulation.

An astounding development has been the proliferation of sensational tabloid newspapers in 1984–85. Some of these seem to have been started by individual entrepreneurs, but most are sponsored by some local government department or social organization, since they have easier access to paper and printing equipment. The papers—as many as eighty are available in Guangzhou—concentrate on sex, murder, and gossip. This "Spiritual Pollution" brought demands for a crackdown, but provincial officials say that the central government cannot ban the newspapers unless they break a specific law, such as publishing pornography or counterrevolutionary articles. Victor Fung of the *Asian Wall Street Journal* surveyed the eighty papers on sale in Guangzhou. He quoted officials as saying there was no illegal material in any of them. However, officials are now insisting on tight registration.

The papers are undoubtedly profitable. In March 1985 one newspaper carrying a long article on Mao's widow, Jiang Qing, sold a million copies in Guangzhou alone for a profit of $10,570—more than the average worker's salary for 34 years (Fung 1985).

Chang Kuo-sin, a veteran Hong Kong journalist who revisited the People's Republic in 1984, says the tabloids open a tiny crack in the state's monopoly of information and distribution. News hawkers reappeared in Kunming for the first time since 1949—all distribution of the media has been handled by various government agencies. "The tabloids are making a much larger crack in China's socialism," Chang said. "They are breaking down the monopoly of the Party press, the monopoly of the ideological press, and they are taking the first steps in establishing an independent press, independent, of course, only in selection of contents and not in expression of editorial opinion—not as yet, anyway" (Chang 1985b,c, 7).

Chang found thirteen tabloids on sale from one vendor. None were from Kunming but were from cities as far away as Changsha, Guiyang, Xian, Kaifeng, Wuzhow, Guilin, and Nanning. This indicates a broad distribution network and a good level of profit for publishers and sellers.

In the papers he examined, Chang found no explicit, lurid

description of sex. Lonely hearts ads and advice columns were frequent, along with racy articles on romance and mystery, sporting headlines such as "Woman lawyer in love with male corpse," "Mystery woman on Moon Lake," and "The swindle that shocked three continents" (Chang 1985a,b).

Control of publications

At the top of the communications pyramid are the central organizations, *The People's Daily,* the Central Broadcasting Station, and Xinhua. These are controlled by the Central Committee of the Chinese Communist party. In turn, they set the approved line for all other publications. When any editor is in doubt, he or she turns to one of the authoritative publications. In times of political trouble, the secondary broadcasters and journals simply reprint stories and editorials verbatim, whether they apply to their special audiences or not. Each organization has the responsibility of monitoring related journals and stations, providing a constant check on what is said publicly throughout the country. And, of course, each municipal or provincial publication is subject to the control of the Party/government committee at its own level.

The Party secretary at each level—provincial, county, commune—must directly supervise all propaganda work, including publishing and broadcasting. The secretary may write editorials, revise articles, organize criticism, start campaigns, and so forth, or may simply appoint people to key positions.

Beyond that, probably the most important means of control is self-control. Regardless of the system, a journalist (or any other official) exercises self-censorship far more often than he or she feels external censorship. Westerners tend to moan at this type of system, but one must remember that American editors are chosen, promoted, and rewarded because they basically agree with the owner of the television station or daily newspaper. In a sense, the editors are using self-censorship in not promoting their own points of view. Similarly, a Communist editor is selected and rewarded because he or she agrees with the owner of the publication—the Communist party.

SELF-CRITICISM

Just as the Western press is supposed to maintain an independent, watchdog function over society, so the Chinese press has been assigned self-criticism, both internally and externally. Self-criticism is practiced first in internal meetings. Second, it shows up in news coverage or editorials. In theory, all the departments of a newspaper may originate articles of this nature within their domain. Third, the letters column carries self-criticism, both for the paper and the rest of society (L. Chu 1982). Chairman Mao (1965, 3:316), the proponent of the practice, said,

Conscientious practice of self-criticism is still another hallmark that distinguishes our Party from all other political parties. As we say, dust will accumulate if a room is not cleaned regularly, our faces will get dirty if they are not washed regularly. Our comrades' minds and our Party's work may also collect dust, and also need sweeping and washing. The proverb "Running water is never stale and a doorhinge is never worm-eaten" means that constant motion prevents the inroads of germs and other organisms.

But difficulties arise from the precarious position of the press. Under the Communist system, the press belongs to the infallible Party, which may not be criticized. Individuals may be criticized, even at the highest level, but only after the Party gives its permission (Hu 1980, 15).

On the question of criticizing responsible cadres, I once told comrades at the newspapers that responsible cadres are after all different from the ordinary cadres. If responsible cadres or high-ranking cadres have made certain mistakes in their work, because of their high position and great responsibility the mistakes will have greater consequences. Whether appropriate or not, criticism of their mistakes will also have greater consequences. The handling of criticism of high-ranking cadres who have committed mistakes is always linked to the whole situation. To resolve a problem concerning the situation requires the Party committee making the decision. *The newspaper cannot make the decision without the Party committee. The newspaper may make the decision first, but it must still consult the Party committee. The Party newspaper cannot act for the Party committee. It is only the Party's assistant, a propaganda and opinion tool under its leadership.* [emphasis added]

Hu Yaobang, the General Secretary of the Chinese Communist

party, used similar language in 1985: "Journalism should reflect what the party and government say, and espouse the party line and government policy. . . . Freedom or rights cannot be separated from responsibilities and obligations. There is no freedom without responsibilities or rights without obligations" (Biddulph 1985, 15). L. Chu (1982, 8) is even more direct: "The rationale is simple indeed: whoever possesses the power decides whom or what to criticize and praise." He cites *Wen Hui Bao* as a good case study.

A popular and independent paper before 1949, *Wen Hui Bao* literally had to copy *The People's Daily* in layout and writing style after Liberation. It lost so much circulation that it closed in 1956. As part of the Hundred Flowers campaign, the paper was reopened a year later. Even though Mao personally complimented the paper for its good job, it was severely criticized when the campaign aborted. The founder, Hsu Chucheng, was called a "rightist" and the paper had to publish a self-criticism and reorganize under the complete control of the Party. Hsu felt the sting of subsequent criticism during the Cultural Revolution and was not rehabilitated until June 1980.

But the story was not over. When Mao Zedong launched the Cultural Revolution, *Wen Hui Bao* joined in vigorously — but on the wrong side. The paper was eventually taken over by the radicals and again had to criticize its own mistakes. But as the flagship of the radical faction, it became the paper that all others had to copy. And to complete the cycle, it had to repudiate its repudiations after the fall of the Gang of Four in 1976 (L. Chu 1982, 10–11).

The People's Daily

The People's Daily is published in the former Beijing Engineering Institute in east Beijing and, although surrounded by walls and fences, the grounds seem to be a cross between a campus and an army post. The staff lives in one compound, which houses some 5,000 workers. This includes journalists, printers, drivers, and cooks — everyone necessary to run a paper and serve its live-in staff.

Most of the buildings are two-story brick. The small offices and editorial rooms have bare tile floors and whitewashed walls; no bull pens here. The quiet reminded Mathews and Mathews (1983, 177) of a "certain insurance-office single-mindedness."

Hu Jiwei, former editor in chief, began his career in Yenan in the thirties. An important editor in the northwest after Liberation, he became deputy editor of *The People's Daily* in the mid-fifties and editor shortly after Mao's death. During the Cultural Revolution he spent several years tending cowpens in Hunan Province, an important political asset today. Hu resigned as director in the fall of 1983. Some sources said this was to protest the fact that Wang Ruoshui had been relieved of his post as deputy editor in charge of theoretical and ideological questions.

Wang believed that both the theory and practice of socialism had yet to be perfected. *The People's Daily* thus became a "liberal" voice carrying a variety of opinions, but all within Marxism-Leninism. His removal was considered a setback for the liberalizing trend in Chinese communism. Qin Chuan, formerly editor in chief, became director.

Internal control of *The People's Daily* today rests with an editorial committee headed by the editor in chief. The five- to ten-member committee gets its instructions from the Party's Central Committee. In turn, the editorial committee decides the paper's policies, chooses personnel, and supervises daily operations of the paper and its associated enterprises. The editor in chief is the chief operating officer, responsible to the editorial committee (Lu 1979/80, 48–49). Reporting to the editor in chief is a deputy editor in chief and a secretary general who supervises all routine work. A director in the office of the editor in chief handles the administrative routines within the editorial division.

The editorial division includes several separate departments, of which the theory and propaganda department is the most important. Its responsibility is to see that "politics takes command"—that the organization always serves the Party. The reporters department supervises correspondents and bureaus in all provinces and municipalities, plus major agricultural and industrial bases.

Other departments include politics and law, rural villages, industry and transportation, finance and economy, culture and education, literature and art, international events, and mass work. The organization is not too different from an American newspaper, with state, national, and city desks and special staffs for business, sports, and life-style. The paper also keeps a domestic and an international morgue for clippings and reference materials.

The literature and art department edits a literary supplement. The international department handles international news, and the eighty-person mass work department answers letters from readers — *The People's Daily* receives 2,000 letters every day (most are referred to other departments; only a few can be printed) (Lu 1979/80, 48–49; An 1981, 25).

Running letters to the editor has its dangers, as the *Liberation Daily* of Shanghai found. In October 1980 the staff asked readers to report cases of power abuses by cadres. Within a month, 13,000 letters inundated the office, while 1,200 people came to complain in person. The bureaucracy reacted so furiously that reporters felt that "sending a report is like committing suicide," according to Mosher (1983, 68–69). Officials showed very little enthusiasm for correcting abuses. Cadres often ignored inquiries or demanded to know who had complained. Some even stormed the newspaper office.

While *The People's Daily* sells for less than a nickel, it made a profit of $25 million in 1980, according to the deputy editor in chief. Such profits belong to the state, but in this case they were being reinvested in other publishing ventures that could benefit China. Both subscriptions and distribution are handled by the post office.

China Daily

China Daily, the first national English-language daily newspaper since 1949, was launched on June 1, 1981, after months of trial runs. Issued simultaneously in China, Hong Kong, and Singapore, it provides foreign residents in China with international and domestic news and Chinese economic and financial information. It helps Chinese students improve their English and strengthens East-West cultural exchanges. It is now available in the United States and can be found in major university libraries.

The paper is printed in Beijing and distributed throughout the country Monday through Saturday. It aims at a circulation of 50,000 and devotes two of its eight pages to advertising. Printed by offset on a good grade of paper, the journal is attractively done in an Australian style, representing the influence of Australian advisers on the project.

Newspaper content

Newspapers were in the hands of extreme Maoists and what became the Gang of Four from 1966 until 1976. During that decade, the papers either "published critiques and theoretical articles that served the cliques' attempts to seize supreme state power, or told about how 'the situation was excellent, and getting better and better'," according to the deputy editor in chief of *The People's Daily*. "They were forbidden to reflect the people's desires and sentiments. At that time, people did not trust the newspapers. In fact, they were reluctant to read them" (An 1981, 25).

The People's Daily is always responsive to the Party's power structure. For example, many letters from readers protested editorials downgrading Zhou En-lai after his death. Lu Ying, who was appointed editor by the Gang of Four, turned their names over to the Gang, and many were jailed. After the fall of the Gang, the staff tried to get releases for everyone who could be located (Mathews and Mathews 1983, 177).

Today, papers are expected to be dedicated to telling the truth—in the words of An Gang (1981, 25), deputy editor in chief of *The People's Daily,* "seeking truth from facts, that is, using practice as the criterion for determining what is right and wrong, reflecting things as they stand, reporting both successes and failures, talking about the bright side as well as the dark side of society and telling the readers both the achievements and difficulties in socialist construction."

This "seeking truth from facts" was not automatically accepted when the Gang of Four was overturned. An Gang cites the 1978 editorial "Practice Is the Only Criterion for Testing Truth" as a turning point. It was published first in *The People's Daily* and then in the regional *Guangming Ribao* and set off a great debate, since the theoretical position of Marxism is that Communist theory is the only criterion. This was especially true of the Cultural Revolution period with its emphasis on the thought of Mao Zedong.

An (1981, 26) concludes, "That debate in a measure has paved the way in the current readjustment of the national economy for criticizing the 'Leftist' mistakes which had prevailed for many years and proceeding with economic work in the light of the realities, possibilities and practical results."

The People's Daily prints eight pages, except on Sunday when it is limited to four. Page one carries top domestic and international news and editorials. Page two is for economics, page three for internal political affairs, culture, education, and social life. More national and international news is on page four. Page five is devoted to theory, academic discussions, literature, and art. Six and seven carry international reports and commentaries, and the eighth page is a literary supplement. About one-third of the seventh and eighth pages is devoted to advertising (Zhou 1981, 23).

At times, local papers did no more than echo the national papers. When the Gang of Four was running things, there was a saying that "the big papers [referring to *The People's Daily* and other national or local papers] copy the small papers [meaning the *Journal of Beijing University* and the *Journal of Tsing Hua University*]; the small papers copy Liang Hsiao [the writers group organized by Jiang Qing at Beijing and Tsin Hua University]." Our studies at the Chinese University in Hong Kong, using every sixth issue of *The People's Daily* and *The Southern Daily* for sixty days of 1980, revealed much more diversity, however (Ip and Wong 1980). Data for the studies are given in Tables 9.1–9.4.

Of the 160 items in *The People's Daily* dealing with the United States, 88 (55 percent) were favorable, 32 unfavorable, and 40 neutral. The unfavorable items were predominantly on foreign relations (12), government and politics (6), the economy (5), and disasters and accidents (4). In *The Southern Daily,* 39

TABLE 9.1. Comparison of news about the United States in two Chinese newspapers during a random sample of sixty days in 1980

Subject	The People's Daily		The Southern Daily	
	Items	Percent of news hole	Items	Percent of news hole
U.S. economy	18	11	4	7
Foreign relations	90	56	31	51
Government, politics	13	8	6	10
Military, defense	13	8	7	11
Social problems	2	1	1	2
Science, medicine	8	5	6	10
Culture, sports	10	6	5	8
Disaster, accidents	5	3	1	2
Race	1	1	. . .	. . .

Note: Percentages do not add to 100 due to rounding.

TABLE 9.2. Amount of news and opinion material in *The People's Daily* and *The Southern Daily*, 1980

	The People's Daily	The Southern Daily
News		
News items	132	60
Percent of news hole	59	98
Opinion		
Items	28	1
Percent of news hole	41	2

TABLE 9.3. News sources for *The People's Daily* and *The Southern Daily*

Source	The People's Daily Percent of news hole	The Southern Daily Percent of news hole
Xinhua	54	70
Own staff	44	12
American paper	1	. . .
No identification[a]	1	17

[a]The unidentified stories were mainly short news items run as "International News in Brief." Apparently from Xinhua, they also appeared in *The People's Daily* with a Xinhua byline.

TABLE 9.4. The United States in *The People's Daily,* January 1979 to November 1980 (alternate weeks)

Subject		Percent of U.S. News Items
Sino-American relations		30.3
Official visits	7.4	
U.S. delegations to China	8.1	
Strengthened diplomatic ties	3.4	
Trade, culture, technology agreements	3.5	
People to people contacts	4.4	
American Taiwan policy	2.3	
Other	1.2	
U.S. domestic news		29.3
Domestic problems		9.2
Social, political	2.4	
Economic	2.5	
Energy crisis	1.9	
Strikes, worker hardships	2.4	
Advanced development		6.0
Science, technology	3.9	
Medicine	1.5	
Agriculture	0.6	
American lifestyle		4.2
Disasters		1.5
Presidential election		4.7
Cabinet appointments		1.5
Sports		1.2
Other		1.0
U.S. foreign policies		39.8
U.S.–Soviet		17.7
U.S. charges aggression in Afghanistan	7.6	
Military race	5.4	
Strategic arms talks	3.2	
Boycott of Soviets	1.5	
Middle East		5.9
Hostages in Iran		5.7
Vietnam, U.S. aid to Thailand		2.7
Other Asian countries		2.7
Cuba		1.5
Other Latin America		1.0
Western Europe		1.2
Eastern Europe		0.1
Others		1.3

Source: Student papers prepared by the author's class in international communication, Chinese University of Hong Kong, fall 1980.

N = 595 items.

items (64 percent) were favorable, 9 unfavorable, and 13 neutral. The 9 unfavorable items were distributed among the economy (4), government and politics (3), and social problems and disasters and accidents (1 each).

For *The People's Daily,* most of the favorable items concerned the U.S. activities against the Soviet Union's invasion of Afghanistan. Unfavorable items were mainly about President Ronald Reagan's views on Taiwan. Neutral items were mainly about U.S.-Iranian relations — generally factual accounts of the hostage situation. However, unfavorable items occupied much more space than favorable ones. A China-centered view of the news is also borne out by the coverage of U.S. economics. The five unfavorable items were comments on inflation and recession, while the favorable stories dealt with economic agreements and, especially, economic sanctions against the Russians.

U.S. sports teams visiting China were hailed as evidence of friendship. But there were other topics such as "How many millionaires in the U.S.?" which concentrated on the great discrepancies between the lives of the rich and the poor. "Cats and dogs enjoy life like a man," was one illustration, while the auction of an old and rare wine for thousands of dollars was another.

Entertainment in *The Southern Daily,* in its broadest definition, accounts for less than 20 percent of the paper. There is a wide fluctuation because the feature page is devoted to a different topic each day. When the topic has to do with culture, sports, or other entertainment, the proportion is high. When the featured topic is on something else, there may be as little as six square inches of entertainment news.

Where papers in Taiwan and Hong Kong publish many reports of the entertainment industry, movies, television, music, and sports, *The Southern Daily* carries only a little sports. Its pictures are not of pretty girls but of art, calligraphy, and artistic photography. Most of the entertainment news reported by Kwok (1980) was composed of literary articles.

10 EDUCATION OF A JOURNALIST

Most Chinese journalists learn their trade on the job, although several journalism courses are now being offered at various teacher's colleges as well as at three main universities. The field is immense, whether one takes the figure of 100,000 professionals plus the nonprofessionals working in wired broadcasting, in rural areas, or as part-time correspondents (Rogers et al. 1985, 187), or the figure of 300,000 reported in the *Beijing Review* (1984, 7). Some journalists are well trained, others only well connected.

Journalism education in Chinese universities was the focus of three students from the Chinese University of Hong Kong who traveled inside China in 1980 and interviewed journalism students. The following is based on their report, which was published in the *Asian Messenger* (Cheung et al. 1982, 61–68).

Journalism facilities

Communist journalism training began in Yenan in the 1930s with the establishment of an anti-Japanese military school that trained some press propaganda cadres for the Red Army. The first official school to offer journalism education was a women's university in Yenan, beginning in 1939.

Immediately after Liberation in 1949, the Communists abolished or reorganized schools built by foreigners, Nationalists, and the bourgeoisie. Most new schools were modeled on the Soviet system. Training emphasized service to the Party and the working class, political theory, language training, and practice.

Most schools were destroyed or closed down during the Cultural Revolution. When they reopened in 1970, entrance exams were abolished in favor of recommendations from communes or factories. Political fervor or personal connections became much more important than ability to do university-level work. This was the case until 1978, when a unified entrance exam was reinstated.

Only print journalism is taught today in the Chinese universities. In 1984 at the university level there were twenty-six journalism departments, thirty-four journalism programs, and one independent academic research center. Another comprehensive institute (including print, broadcasting, and film) was being planned for Beijing. (A *Beijing Review* article in May 1985 stated that 2,800 students were studying journalism in twenty-six colleges and universities.)

The main programs in 1985 were those at Jinan University in Guangzhou, Fudan University in Shanghai, People's University in Beijing, the Beijing Broadcasting Institute, and Xiamen University.

JINAN UNIVERSITY

Jinan has been graduating students only since 1982. Before the Cultural Revolution, journalism was a professional training course under the Chinese-language faculty. During the Cultural Revolution, the school was occupied by the army and forced to close. When it reopened in 1978, a faculty of journalism was appointed for a four-year course. In 1981, there were 144 students in the first three years, since a senior class had not yet gone through the curriculum. One-third of the student body was from Hong Kong or Macao. The university has no graduate school since it has been open such a short time. It is the only Chinese university open to overseas Chinese students.

FUDAN UNIVERSITY

Fudan, the oldest of the group, was founded in 1929. It has gradually absorbed other journalism institutes in Shanghai, building a strong faculty by 1952. Because of newspaper attacks during the Cultural Revolution, the journalism faculty suspended operations for two years. In 1970 it reopened, admitting students by recommendation rather than examination.

In 1981 the school had no graduate school, but graduate students were independently attached to the faculty. I met several who were doing M.A. theses on some facet of American journalism, although their resources left much to be desired. There were 229 undergraduates and nine graduate students. Some seventy graduates leave the school each year. Fudan publishes an academic journal called *Journalism University*.

PEOPLE'S UNIVERSITY AND BEIJING UNIVERSITY

The People's University was the first socialist university founded after the establishment of the People's Republic of China. It was an outgrowth of the North China University and a consolidation of several wartime schools that specialized in training Party cadres. The university was founded in 1950.

The People's University set up its own journalism faculty in 1955, with most of its students coming from cadres training in the propaganda department. The faculty was combined with the journalism training course of Beijing University in 1960. Between 1968 and 1978, however, the university was taken over by the medical university, and faculty and students were transferred to Beijing University as part of the Chinese-language faculty. But in September 1978 the department returned to its mother school. The school's journal is called *The World Press*.

CURRICULUM

Each university offers a four-year curriculum leading to a degree roughly similar to a B.A. Students have a major but no minor and few electives. Beginning in 1980, Fudan adopted a credit-hour system under which a student needs 144 credits to graduate, including 112 credits in compulsory subjects and 32 in electives.

Wall Newspaper – Students at Fudan University stop to read the latest news (*Fudan University,* a brochure published by the university in 1978). Located in Shanghai, the university was founded in 1905. It has one of the most advanced departments of journalism. Since China is short of machinery and technology, unconventional media such as big character posters have been used effectively along with an interpersonal network that extends the influence of the Party and the government to every person in China.

Journalism training appears to be a priority with the Chinese government. Educational centers are planned for every province. Increasing literacy, urbanization, and responsibility for economic performance will demand a great increase in the mass media (especially in publications, films, and broadcasts for vocational and special-interest groups). While salaries are low and personal risk for political mistakes is always in a writer's mind, journalists are afforded relatively high social status.

The curriculum is divided into three major categories. The first is political theory, including political economy, the history of the Chinese Communist party, and the history and philosophy of the international Communist movement. In mid-1985 the required courses in Marxism were slashed generally by 25 to 40 percent. "We want our students to have the ability to solve problems practically — revolution isn't everything," Beijing University president Ding Shisun was quoted as saying (*Atlanta Journal-Constitution* 1985b). The second category includes theories of journalism news gathering and writing, editing, and the history of newspapers or the history of journalism. The third element is the basic course, which aims at strengthening general knowledge. It includes grammar, rhetoric, classical and modern literature, history and geography, international affairs, foreign languages, and physical education.

As Table 10.1 indicates, Fudan's core courses are more numerous than those of the People's University and Jinan and offer greater variety. On the other hand, the Jinan faculty is more cosmopolitan, since 40 percent of its students come from overseas. Students can easily get foreign news and read foreign newspapers and magazines that are not available at other universities. Jinan also has a course on international affairs that

TABLE 10.1. Compulsory journalism courses, 1980

Course	Fudan University	People's University	Jinan University
Introduction to journalism	*		
Theory of journalism	*	*	*
History of Chinese journalism	*	*	*
News gathering and writing	*	*	*
Newspaper and people's work	*	*	*
Editing	*	*	
Basic writing	*	*	*
News translation	*	*	*
Western journalism	*		
Management of the foreign press	*	*	*
Photojournalism	*	*	*
Newspaper reading and comment		*	*
International affairs			*
Special topics	*	*	*
Publications practicum	*		*
Internship	*	*	*
Research on journalism theory	*		
Critique of student work	*		

discusses some current events such as happenings in Iran and Afghanistan, the energy crisis, the international monetary system, and the American general elections. Jinan invites journalists from Hong Kong and Macao and hopes to offer a course in legal systems, a pioneering step.

Each school offers fieldwork or internships. The systems at Fudan and Jinan are quite similar, with two fieldwork periods. One takes up two months of the second year, when students are placed as interns on the municipal papers. The second field period takes four months of the fourth year, when students are sent to the provincial press. The People's University offers one fieldwork session, five months during the third year. Students also act as correspondents for newspapers.

Only Jinan has a laboratory newspaper for students. Called *Student News,* it concentrates on college news, with some discussion of journalism theory and occasional reports of outside news and literary works. As of 1981, Fudan had no student newspaper, but the faculty was expected to take over the editorial work of the Fudan University paper. Beijing University occasionally publishes an experimental magazine called *Morning,* but only two issues had been published by 1981.

People's University published two literary magazines in 1981, *University Students* and *New Earth.* Only about 100 copies of each issue were run off. *University Students* lasted three issues and *New Earth* came out only once.

Journalism courses do not use textbooks. Teachers lecture and students take notes. Sometimes mimeographed notes are available, and there are some reference books compiled by other journalism faculties and organizations. But the faculty have not been eager to commit themselves to paper. Politics is to blame for this situation (Cheung et al. 1982, 66):

Following factional struggles, the contents of materials are subject to constant revisions. Take, for example, the students graduating in 1981. When they studied in the first year, their course on journalism theory was different from that of the 1981 freshman students. Under these circumstances, the university has neither the chance to revise and publish a set of fixed and systematic teaching materials, nor the intention to spend time on this, lest it may be changed again in the next political upheaval. For self-protection, many teachers do not dare to publish materials for fear that they may offend the existing authorities.

Examinations are held at the end of each four-month term. Beijing University, for example, uses conventional letter grades for most subjects but only a pass-fail grade for the history of China and ancient Chinese literature.

None of the schools is well equipped. The People's University was heavily damaged during the Cultural Revolution, though it does have a reference room and access to the library of Beijing University, the second largest in China. People's University has a darkroom, more than 100 cameras, an editorial room, and typewriters. Fudan is by far the best equipped. It has more than twenty English typewriters, some fifty cameras, and a dozen tape recorders. There are eight air-conditioned darkrooms with photo printers and enlargers. The department has four special classrooms and two reference rooms. Jinan has a small reference room, but better publications. It has only a poorly equipped, makeshift darkroom.

FACULTY

The People's University has more than forty teachers and twenty staff members. The teachers are all university graduates but have no graduate degrees, and most have no journalism experience. Fudan has thirty-one teachers, including two professors, seven assistant professors, and twenty-two lecturers. Most are graduates of its own journalism faculty and have worked as editors or reporters. Jinan has more than thirty teachers, most of them experienced reporters. About twenty journalists from Hong Kong and Macao have given guest lectures in a two-year period.

Usually two or three similar subjects are combined to form a "teaching and research group," somewhat like an American department or sequence. Within the unit, some teachers are responsible for teaching and others for research and the improvement of teaching methods. The People's University has five such units, including journalism theory, journalism management, news gathering and writing, and editing and photojournalism. Fudan has six such units. Social science research methods were abolished during the Cultural Revolution and are just now gingerly being reintroduced. The most advanced technique I heard of during my visit in 1980–81 was an elementary content analysis of American newspaper and newsmagazine advertising. Most teachers are former practitioners who are not interested in academic research.

JOB PROSPECTS

Jobs are controlled by the university. Graduates are usually sent to newspapers at either the central, provincial, or municipal level. An effort is made to send the student to his or her native province, but the needs of the press are primary. The graduate may object to an assignment, and occasionally a change is made. But once on the job, the journalist is probably stuck (or set) for life. Students proficient in foreign languages, including graduates from foreign-language departments, are chosen for special training at the Academy of Social Science and placed at Xinhua or other press units using foreign languages.

According to a Jinan graduate, starting salaries for university graduates are higher than for secondary school graduates. During their first year, which is probationary, the university graduates receive 51 ren min bi (RMB) or yuan, or about $60; the secondary school graduate, 36. For the second year, the figures are 61.5 vs. 41 or 42 RMB. Salaries fluctuate according to local standards of living. There is no fixed or guaranteed promotion system, but reporters do enjoy a high social status.

Broadcasting education

The institution for broadcast education is the Beijing Broadcasting Institute, founded in 1959. It offers a four-year undergraduate program and a three-year graduate course. Most of its emphasis is on engineering and technical operations, but it does offer work for editors and correspondents (Beijing Broadcasting Institute 1980).

Seriously damaged and closed down during the Cultural Revolution, the institute now has 864 students and a staff of 630, including 197 on the faculty. It has a library of 300,000 books, plus 500 periodicals, laboratories, experimental broadcasting facilities, and housing.

The institute has six departments: journalism, literature and art editing, announcing for television, radio engineering, and foreign languages. There are four basic teaching sections: theory of Marxism-Leninism, Chinese language and literature, a combined course in mathematics and physical chemistry, and physical culture. The journalism department teaches editing and commentary, tape-recorded reports, broadcast history, and news broadcasting theory. The literature and art editing department teaches writing, music editing, and editing of dramatic productions. The announcing department teaches sound production and announcing. The television department covers TV photography, directing, and film editing. Courses include music, art, introduction to films and tapes, photographic design, camera work, film editing, conducting, performing, and analysis of films. Radio engineering covers radio, television, and microwave engineering and television control center operations. The foreign language department offers only English. Most of its courses are for students in other departments. Each department offers its own basic courses. The liberal arts include Communist theory, international relations, theory of literature and art, ancient and modern Chinese literature, foreign literature, English, and physical education.

The institute offers various courses of in-service training to broadcasters from the central, provincial, and municipal levels. It also sponsors a Research Institute of Journalism for the study of news broadcasting in foreign countries. It maintains an active program on publications. The institute has about 3,000 alumni and is projecting a student body of 2,500 to 3,000 by the end of the 1980s, with a faculty of 600. The following goals for institute students are found in Beijing Broadcasting Institute (1980):

Students should support the leadership of the Chinese Communist Party, love their motherland and be imbued with the spirit of devoting themselves to the construction of modernization, with fine moral sense. They should grasp the basic theory, special knowledge and skills which their respective specialties require, and they should keep abreast of the latest scientific achievements and trends as much as they can; they should have the ability of self-analyzing and self-solving problems. Students should learn the way of making scientific researches and social investigations; master one kind of foreign languages; be of strong constitutions. These are the general aims of the Beijing Broadcasting Institute in training its students.

Graduate studies

The Graduate School of the Chinese Academy of Social Sciences offers work in philosophy, economics, history, literature, journalism, and 102 professions. The journalism sequence is housed in *The People's Daily* compound and is made up principally of students recruited from other disciplines, such as economics or foreign languages. It was founded in 1978 and graduated its first class in September 1981 after a three-year course of study (*Asian Messenger* 1982, 4). These students are assigned jobs overseas and in the leading journalistic institutions.

Journalism conference

China's first journalism education conference was held in Beijing in May and June 1983 (Centre for Contemporary Asian Studies 1983, 4). The conferees proposed that China will need some 110,000 journalists who are university graduates. At least 5,000 should be trained annually. They also recommended that at least one journalism department at a higher education institute be formed for each large region. China hoped to launch her first college of journalism in 1984 and to expand from sixteen to thirty key journalism centers by 1990.

11 PAST ACHIEVEMENT, FUTURE CHANGE

Chinese paintings are highly symbolic. A landscape is not just a pretty picture, though it outlines an interesting journey. The scene has major philosophical implications, based on a combination of Taoism and Confucianism. Artists and philosophers find in nature the same law and order they believe governs the heavens and men when rulers follow heaven's mandate. The scroll *Streams and Mountains without End* illustrates both Chinese painting and a Chinese view of history. Seven feet long, it is viewed from right to left. The painting begins with a gentle *andante* passage, building to a climactic new theme in mountains and village. Just as a symphony might do, the painting then fades into a quiet but strong and rolling section, climaxing again with a variation of the mountains seen earlier. This section recalls the past and prepares for the future. Sharp vertical cliffs make the next section very staccato, followed by a rocky variation leading to the great finale. Mountains boil and seethe, almost like flowing lava. The composition ends with a reprise of the opening movement, adding the mountainous elements that have dominated the entire piece. This unifies conflicting elements and summarizes the entire scroll (Lee n.d., 348–51).

In a similar way, Chinese history has always been marked by thrust and counterthrust, sometimes with the vigor of a kung fu movie but more often with the subtlety of calligraphy. Dynasty succeeds dynasty, drought follows flood, and ocean barbarians succeed foreign devils, but the immutable essence of China remains.

China and her communication system must and will change, just as streams give way to mountains and mountains to streams. New leaders with their own priorities will follow this generation, but China and her communication system will remain socialist and authoritarian. A violent change, either toward Maoism or capitalism, is unlikely.

Achievements of the Mao communication system

What successes can the old Maoist system claim? First, the highly personal propaganda system of the Chinese Communist party raised revolutionary consciousness. It made an oppressed people aware of its own misery, aware that most oppression is man-made, mandate of heaven or no. Through decades of struggle and patient education, the Communists demonstrated that men do not have to live like sheep and die like dogs. Their propaganda differed fundamentally from that of earlier Chinese revolutions by being almost entirely personal and oral and directed toward peasants. Earlier Chinese revolution had been primarily for the educated city dweller. By force of circumstance, the Communists found their following among illiterate peasants.

Second, the system proved its worth in battle. From today's perspective, the wars of the thirties, forties, and fifties were not highly technological. Infantry, a human sea of soldiers inspired to fight and die for their country, was decisive.

In fighting the Kuomintang and the Japanese, Communist soldiers were self-sufficient. They grew their own food, manufactured many of their own weapons, and carried supplies on their own backs. Only in Korea did modern supplies and a reasonably elaborate procurement and supply system become necessary. Therefore, a simple communication system was sufficient. But missiles, satellites, and economic warfare do not lend themselves so easily to mass meetings and field telephones.

The system can claim more successes than just in the military field, however. Certainly the communication system deserves some credit for guiding immense changes in China's economic and political organization. Initial Communist penetration of the country was forcible, of course, but an enormous job had to be done to establish day-to-day control. Government presence was often minuscule, but even a minimal presence in a million cities, towns, and villages is an awe-inspiring performance.

Selling the economic and political program was even more difficult. To have land reform, for example, peasants had to be convinced that their grievances were legitimate and the heavens would not fall at the sound of their complaints. Thousands of "struggle" meetings had to be painstakingly arranged. Once the "rich" peasants were deposed, there was an information campaign aimed at forming communes.

The system's promotion of the Mao myth was so successful that it withstood even the monumental failure of the Great Leap Forward, and the Cultural Revolution's messianic fervor accounted for both achievements and excesses. Nor was the system entirely one-way. Some credit for warning against the disasters of the commune movement, the Great Leap Forward, and more recently, the Spiritual Pollution campaign should go to the communication system.

The Maoist system was a hierarchical one that worked best in emergencies, mobilizing against real or supposed threats from foreign devils or class enemies. It was built on an essentially emotional appeal, with only a veneer of rational analysis. The hierarchical system is suited to command, warfare, and national emergencies, but it is weak in several respects: Downward communication tends to become distorted after passing through two or three levels, upward communication tends to be slanted to please the commander, and lateral communication is severely limited except as informal channels (such as the networks of relatives or ex–Red Guards) supplements the formal system.

Perhaps the most important factor in the Cultural Revolution was that it depended upon what the Chinese call a cult of personality—the deification of Chairman Mao. Every experienced propagandist, whether evangelist or advertiser, attempts to personify good and evil. Abstractions are almost impossible to sell to the masses. Personal heroes who save us from personal villains are much easier to understand.

The series of meetings held in Beijing so that young people could meet Chairman Mao served the same function as religious camp meetings in nineteenth-century America. From the inspirational pageants in Beijing the new apostles went forth to spread the word of the chairman's struggle with evil, as personified by his opponents.

Mao seems always to have deliberately appealed to the unsophisticated. In the Cultural Revolution, he aimed primarily at the young and immature. He started a campaign filled with drama and excitement, playing upon the universal desire of teenagers to rebel and to establish their independence. Teachers, policemen, parents—all authority figures—were subjugated to the tyranny of youth.

Apparently, not many careerists were on the right side at the beginning of the Cultural Revolution, but the movement offered incredible opportunities for advancement, and young people were quick to seize them. Born too late to be heroes of the military revolution, or even of the struggle in Korea, they could avoid a long climb up the ladder by riding the elevator of political zeal.

The Cultural Revolution depended partly on internal threats. The Great Leap Forward had failed, people said, because of traitors. All China's problems could be solved simply by applying Chairman Mao's thought (simple solutions are always popular favorites). The confidence of China's young people was also greatly strengthened by their long isolation from the rest of the world—they had nothing with which to compare the movement's promises.

Still another factor in the success of the Cultural Revolution was the fact that it offered a chance to settle old factional and personal scores. The possibility that today's winner is tomorrow's loser did not figure in anyone's calculations.

The movement depended heavily on seizing communication networks, both media and interpersonal. The first targets were radio stations and newspapers, although the People's Liberation Army quickly took control of broadcasting away from the radicals. Then in every commune, housing unit, and factory the interpersonal network was seized by young activists with their interminable meetings. Actually, the Cultural Revolution set a relatively simple task—throw the rascals out! No thought was given to production, distribution, and education, and very little even to elementary government, so a simple communication system was good enough.

The failures of the Maoist communication system are apparent from the Cultural Revolution's very successes: The system was too open downward to manipulation by small groups such as the Gang of Four; it was deficient in reporting upward; and lateral information was often missing, distorted, or completely misleading. Not enough reliable information was available for the sophisticated planning necessary for China's industrialization and emergence as a world power.

Post-Mao communications

The year 1985, the Year of the Ox, marked gathering economic reform, which necessarily means change in the political and media systems, including interpersonal, nonofficial channels.

Modern China faces immense informational difficulties. A peasant economy may require only a primitive communication system, but factory planners need to know about long-range political plans; long- and short-range forecasts of domestic and foreign markets; other factories' plans; the availability of capital, labor, raw materials, transportation, distribution channels, and advertising media; and a host of other factors. Unfortunately, many of these informational needs have not been met. Travel and tourism is becoming a major industry in China, for example, but an easing of the regulations on domestic travel has clogged trains and hotels because programs to promote tourism overseas were not coordinated with those to build hotels or train staffs. No one in China had seen a bellboy for thirty-five years, much less organized an electronic reservation system. In short, many managerial problems have proved to be informational problems.

Interpersonal networks must also improve. Official networks run along organizational lines, for example, between cadres responsible for the Young Pioneers in the various provinces, or along lines of blood and/or patronage. These must at least make room for networks of technicians based on common problems rather than party organization or personal obligation.

The government is moving to reduce its direct control of economic institutions, probably because guiding every factory and farm in such an immense nation is beyond any government's ability. The government and Communist ideology will still control the economy and set basic plans, but individual and corporate responsibility will be stressed. Informational and other managerial problems will still exist, but the man on the job will have a better chance of solving them than a bureaucrat in Beijing.

These changes threaten the established bureaucracy; entrepreneurs, economic czars, and international traders do not spring from the ranks of battle-scarred revolutionaries. As a Hong Kong journalist put it, "China has saddled herself with a task which her leaders are not fit to perform. The leaders may be and actually are professionals in revolution, in guerrilla warfare, but they are amateurs or novices in administration and in the running of corporate business" (Chang 1984). From this realization springs China's great interest in education and recruiting new technicians while forcing the retirement of old cadres.

Economic changes have only been possible because of ideological changes, beginning with a few cautious steps toward dissociating Mao from the extremes of the Gang of Four, and indeed from his own post-1949 Luddism. The media also contributed to this movement. The editorial "Practice Is the Only Criterion for Testing Truth," published in *The People's Daily* in 1978, is cited as the turning point in a shift from ideology to pragmatism. The availability of uncensored reports through *neibu* must also have been effective, and the immigrants in our study demonstrate the influence of an interpersonal network.

Inevitably there have been reactions. Sensationalistic tabloids and video peep shows are more than many can bear. And the responsibility system has not worked very well in manufacturing, which depends on many variables the individual factory cannot control.

The future of the Chinese communication systems

Probably China has gone too far for a full retreat, except in reaction to a severe threat. An economic disaster would certainly mean a setback, and China is still susceptible to drought, flood, gluts in the market, and mismanagement. Certainly China's economic revolution has been much better managed than that of most of the Third World; perhaps she has more to teach than we thought. But even a temporary setback probably would not bring back a radical regime. The population is now much more sophisticated, and it would be hard to launch a real ideological crusade.

And the economic policy is working. This generation did not experience the bitter times before the revolution, but it is very much aware that people's lives have improved—not steadily, but in fits and starts—since the overthrow of the Gang of Four.

We may well see more restrictions placed on the media. Criticism of the foundations of the state and the Party have always been off-limits. Practically all publishing is now done by official organs of state or Party, and these may be brought into line on the issues of sensationalism and pornography (although incorporating Hong Kong will raise new questions here as well).

As basic needs for security are fulfilled, communication systems will move to fill the "higher" needs such as sex, love, and acceptance, followed by motives of self-esteem and competence—curiosity, achievement, and organization (McKeachie and Doyle 1966, 221–22).

Under the stress of war and purges, the Chinese used the media for survival. Newspapers were carefully read to discover "safe" opinions and successful officials. But 1984 saw the phenomenon of tabloid newspapers, consisting almost entirely of light-headed entertainment.

Early radio consisted mainly of ideological music, exhortations from Chairman Mao's sayings, and reminders of quotas, meetings, and other activities necessary for survival. Television followed the same pattern with Jiang Qing's revolutionary operas, but immediately after the downfall of the Gang of Four television became slightly more entertaining and a good deal more helpful educationally. By 1985 a considerable part of the day's programs were pure entertainment, including foreign films and imported cartoon series.

The same movement may be seen in book publishing. The early emphasis was on scientific and technical works. During the Cultural Revolution, little was published but propaganda promoting the new revolution. Now classical literature, dating manuals, and even comic books are available. In short, we will see more of the human side of an authoritarian state, though it will remain authoritarian for decades.

Not everything old is bad, nor is everything new good. Schell (1984, 79) makes a strong case for keeping some collective values: "In many areas of China, Maoist collectivization was not a debacle. Analysts of China's economy generally agree that collectivization worked well in about a third of China's communes, had mixed results in a third, and was a disaster in the last third."

Some areas where the responsibility system is not working well include the Five Guarantees (social welfare), agricultural mechanization, basic grain production, collectivized medicine, police, and public works like irrigation. These problems are solvable, of course, but not yet. David Bonavia, correspondent of the London *Times,* says, "The Chinese are pretty much meandering across a new landscape in the fog" (Schell 1984, 90). Liang and Shapiro (1984, 112–14) report that the popular arts are thriving. But elite tastes or troupes representing impoverished areas have had to appeal for socialist subsidies.

Finally, some enterprises have found that freedom includes freedom to fail. Officials had warned some forty inefficient factories that they would be allowed to fail. Some shook up management and became profitable. But in August 1986 the Shenyang Explosion Proof Equipment Factory had the dubious honor of becoming the first Communist enterprise to go into formal bankruptcy. Workers and management alike were devastated by loss of face and loss of a guaranteed career, although they were given limited unemployment compensation (Fung 1986, 1, 16).

Opportunities

The road Chinese communicators have traveled has wound around like a path through the mountains portrayed in *Streams and Mountains without End*. Now the People's Republic is ready for the relatively peaceful section of the scroll that repeats and unites the elements of the entire painting. But journalistic and artistic opportunities are limited by basic facts. Literacy and low income levels restrain media growth, especially in the country. Telephones, for example, are still relatively rare in rural areas, and until community satellite dishes become much more common, television will be slow to penetrate sparsely populated areas. Reading remains an urban pastime.

Linguistic differences also continue to hinder communications. There is a growing trend toward regional publishing houses, movie studios, and radio and television broadcasting, partly to emphasize local concerns but largely because people are much more comfortable in their own dialect. The government drive for complete assimilation, using Mandarin as its main tool, seems to have been muted.

Overseas distribution of information is still hampered, both by the multiplicity of dialects and a simplified set of characters that is not universally adopted. The lack of foreign exchange hinders imports, including that of media.

Geography is a major obstacle. New roads, railroads, and airlines will help the nonbroadcast media, but these massive undertakings are only a small beginning. Broadcasting, of course, is much easier now that the Chinese have their own satellite system, which could broadcast to all of Southeast Asia.

Xinhua could be a major contributor to the New World Information Order if it can shake off its ethnocentrism. The agency has one of the world's largest information-gathering systems but only a small distribution system. The entire nation's output consists of six magazines, *The China Daily,* a small news report in English, shortwave broadcasts, and a few books and motion pictures. Xinhua could deliver news, photos, and broadcast material via satellite if it had the training and desire.

Changing demographics will provide new challenges and opportunities. The population will continue to grow for several decades, even if the family planning program is completely successful. In the long run, however, China will face an aging population with a greatly decreased work force, and this change in the audience mix will be reflected in media content.

For the foreseeable future, a great hunger for education and entertainment remains unfilled. We can expect a boom in educational and self-educational products across the entire spectrum, while novels, entertaining movies and broadcast programs, nightclubs, and recreational facilities are in great demand.

The only way to advance has been to join the Party or the army. Now other paths are opening. This tends to unleash individual potential, including that of journalists and publishers.

There should be a great growth of regional and ethnic journalism, film, and education. Probably there will be less centralized control, but what remains may be more effective because of better communication and transportation. Contributing to regional development is the policy of controlled urbanization. Cities grew tremendously after 1949, but urbanization is now pretty well controlled. As increased farming efficiency makes them unnecessary, the government has a policy of relocating peasants in new factories and services in the smaller cities and towns (Goldstein and Goldstein 1984). According to an Associated Press dispatch of February 2, 1985, officials expect to move 180 million rural workers out of a total of 450 million off the farm by the year 2000, and this will certainly open up more media opportunities.

As discussed earlier, China may expect some growth in exports. Because of linguistic and cultural differences, however, this growth will be less in cultural products than in television receivers, printing, and other products in which inexpensive production outweighs the considerable cost of transportation and basic communication.

Film exports and coproductions are growing. Between 1980

and 1983, China sold 2,131 films to 105 countries and regions, according to Zen Desheng, a deputy director of the China Film Export and Import Corporation (Zhu 1984). In 1984 the Chinese expected to import more than sixty foreign films, mainly from Britain, the United States, and France, and as of the spring of 1985 the China Film Co-production Corporation had made some eighty films with foreign producers (*Beijing Review* 1985, 31).

Printing should also prove profitable to the Chinese, except that printing is now one of the most automated industries. Low costs in the People's Republic are partially offset by difficulties in quality control and high shipping costs. Chinese newspapers are rather cheaply produced, but some book and magazine work is quite superior.

In any case, the Chinese must learn to be audience centered and market driven, both for export and for the domestic market. Relative affluence and freedom to choose will mean that products the government deems to be good for people will be swamped by products people want to buy. One can hardly have a central plan for culture.

Finally, there are great possibilities for Chinese journalists and other media craftsmen. They have taken much more than that first step with which the longest journey begins. The People's Republic has not come to the end of the scroll of *Streams and Mountains without End,* for the end is also the beginning. But perhaps it has survived the mountain crags to enjoy the foothills, if not the lush valley.

REFERENCES CITED

Abrams, Jim. 1986. Giant strides made in post-Mao decade. *South China Morning Post,* September 1.

An Gang. 1981. Mouthpiece of the people. *Beijing Review,* May 18.

Asian Messenger. 1981a. County Papers. Winter.

———. 1981b. Movie magazines. Winter.

———. 1981c. New themes in Chinese movies. Winter.

———. 1981d. Chinese publications. Winter.

———. 1982. Too many pretty girls. Spring.

Atlanta Journal-Constitution. 1984. Millions died from famine, China admits. September 12.

———. 1985a. China moves from fields into cities. February 2.

———. 1985b. China relaxes political study rule. June 8.

———. 1987. Two top Chinese science officials are fired after student protest. January 23.

Atwood, L. Erwin, and N. Lin. 1982. Cankao Xiaoxi: News for China's cadre. *Journalism Quarterly,* 59, no. 2.

Barnett, A. Doak. 1967. *Cadres, Bureaucracy, and Political Power in Communist China.* New York: Columbia University Press.

Beijing Broadcasting Institute. 1980. Brief introduction to the Beijing Broadcasting Institute.

Beijing Review. 1981. Fifty militant years. November 23.

———. 1984a. Chinese telephones cause headache. November 19.

———. 1984b. Newsmen awarded at media meeting. December 17.

———. 1985a. Communications boom expected. February 18.

———. 1985b. State Statistical Bureau communique on fulfillment of China's 1984 economic and social development plan. March 25.

———. 1985c. Children press grows. June 17.

_____. 1985d. Film statistics for 1984.

Bernstein, Thomas P. 1985. China in 1984: The year of Hong Kong. *Asian Survey,* vol. 25, no. 1.

Biddulph, Jim. 1985. Peking is seducing the Hong Kong press. *Asian Wall Street Journal Weekly,* May 13.

Bishop, Robert L. 1966. The overseas branch of the Office of War Information. Unpublished Ph.D. dissertation, University of Wisconsin, Madison.

_____. 1983. *Economics, Politics and Information.* Ann Arbor: University Microfilm International.

Brandt, Conrad, Benjamin Schwartz, and John K. Fairbank. 1952. *A Documentary History of Chinese Communism, 1921–1950.* Cambridge: Harvard University Press.

Britton, Roswell S. 1933. *The Chinese Periodical Press, 1800–1912.* Shanghai: Kelly and Walsh.

Butterfield, Fox. 1982. *China, Alive in the Bitter Sea.* New York: Time Books.

_____. 1987. U.S. sees setback for China's plans of modernization. *New York Times,* January 15, 1.

Centre for Contemporary Asian Studies. 1983. Chinese journalism education needs reform. *CCAS Newsletter,* Autumn.

Chan, Anita, Richard Madsen, and Jonathan Unger. 1984. *Chen Village: The Recent History of a Peasant Community in Mao's China.* Berkeley: University of California Press.

Chang Kuo-sin. 1985a. The triflers of truth. *Hong Kong Standard,* January 23.

_____. 1985b. A Chinese opinion: Non-conformist publications seen in Kunming. *Hong Kong Standard,* April 2.

_____. 1985c. Beijing fears spread of tabloids. *Hong Kong Standard,* April 9.

_____. 1985d. Beijing's ban on tabloids not justified. *Hong Kong Standard,* April 16.

Chen Bo. 1985. Popular, realistic new films. *China Reconstructs,* February.

Chen Ta. 1940. *Emigrant Communities in South China.* New York: Institute of Pacific Relations.

Chen Yu-tung. 1952. Liquidation of the old legal view as a condition for thorough implementation of the marriage law. *Hsin Chung-Kuo Fu-nu (New Chinese Women),* no. 9. In C. K. Yang, 1965, *Chinese Communist Society: The Family and the Village.* Cambridge: MIT Press.

Cheung Kit-fung, Chow Wai-sheung, and Yim Pui-hang. 1982. Journalism education in China's universities since 1978. *The Asian Messenger,* Spring.

China Business Review. 1985.

China Daily. 1985. June 8.

China Pictorial. 1979. The voice and the strength of the people: The Tian an men Square incident of 1976. Vol. 1.

Chu, Godwin C., ed. 1978a. *Popular Media in China: Shaping New Cultural Patterns.* Honolulu: University of Hawaii Press.

———. 1978b. *Radical Change through Communication in Mao's China.* Honolulu: University of Hawaii Press.

Chu, Godwin C., and Francis L. K. Hsu. 1979. *Moving a Mountain: Cultural Change in China.* Honolulu: University of Hawaii Press.

———. 1983. *China's New Social Fabric.* London: Kegan Paul.

Chu, James. 1982. Advertising in China: Its policy, practice and evolution. *Journalism Quarterly,* vol. 59, no. 1.

Chu, Leonard. 1979/80. Advertising returns to China. *The Asian Messenger,* Winter/Spring.

———. 1980/81. Changing faces of China's TV. *The Asian Messenger,* Winter/Spring.

———. 1982. Press criticism and self-criticism in Communist China: An analysis of its ideology, structure, and operation. Unpublished paper presented to the Association for Education in Journalism, Athens, Ohio, July 25–28.

Daniels, Robert V. 1962. *A Documentary History of Communism,* vol. 2. New York: Random House (Vintage Books).

Dong Wenfang. 1984. TV universities. *China Reconstructs,* November.

Falkenheim, Victor C. 1978. Political participation in China. *Problems of Communism,* May/June.

Fan Zhilong. 1981. China's best-sellers and how they are made. *China Reconstructs,* April.

Fung, Victor. 1985. Proliferation of racy Chinese tabloids kindles fear of crackdown by Peking. *Asian Wall Street Journal Weekly,* June 3.

———. 1986. A Chinese factory falls prey to that byproduct of capitalism—Failure. *Asian Wall Street Journal Weekly,* August 4.

Gargan, Edward A. 1987a. Chinese editorials suggest protests have hit the limits. *New York Times,* January 7.

———. 1987b. China Premier vows to limit campaign against dissent. *New York Times,* January 30.

———. 1987c. Some Chinese leaders favoring old Soviet plans. *New York Times,* February 13.

Goldstein, Sidney, and Alice Goldstein. 1984. Population movement: Labor force absorption and urbanization in China. *Annals of the American Academy of Political and Social Science,* November.

Hong Kong Standard. 1986. Cartoonists with little originality. September 1.

Howkins, John. 1982. *Mass Communication in China.* New York and London: Longman.

Hsu, Immanuel C.-Y. 1983. *The Rise of Modern China,* 3rd ed. New York: Oxford University Press.

Hu Chi-wei. 1980. Treat and study press criticism as an academic question. *News Front,* December. (Quoted in L. Chu 1982)

Huan Xiang. 1985. On reform of Chinese economic structure. *Beijing Review,* May 20.

Ip Wing Chung and Wong Tak Yuen. 1980. U.S. image projected by two Communist Chinese newspapers. Unpublished paper, Chinese University of Hong Kong.

Kaiser, Robert G. 1976. *Russia: The People and the Power.* New York: Pocket Books.

Ko Kung-chen. 1931. *Chung-Kuo Pao-Hsueh Shih (History of Chinese Journalism).* Shanghai.

Kwok Tat Chun. 1980. The entertainment aspects of newspapers in China, Taiwan and Hong Kong. Unpublished paper, Chinese University of Hong Kong.

Lee, Chin-Chuan. 1981. The United States as seen through *The People's Daily. Journal of Communication,* vol. 31, no. 4.

Lee Sherman E. n.d. *A History of Far Eastern Art.* New York: Prentice-Hall.

Liang Heng and Judith Shapiro. 1983. *Son of the Revolution.* New York: Knopf.

———. 1984. *Intellectual Freedom in China after Mao, with a Focus on 1983.* New York: Fund for Free Expression.

———. 1986. *After the Nightmare.* New York: Knopf.

Liang Shu-ming. 1932. *Chung-kuo min-tsu tzu-chiu yun-tung chui-hou chichueh-wu (The Final Awakening of the Chinese National Self-salvation Movement).* Peking. In C. K. Yang, 1965, *Chinese Communist Society: The Family and The Village.* Cambridge: MIT Press.

Lieberthal, Kenneth. 1984. China's political reforms: A net assessment. *Annals of the American Academy of Political and Social Science,* November.

Lin Yutang. 1936. *A History of the Press and Public Opinion in China.* Chicago: University of Chicago Press. (Printed in China by Kelly and Walsh)

Ling Yang. 1981. China's burgeoning TV. *Beijing Review,* March 9.

———. 1982. Broadcasting serves the people. *Beijing Review,* February 22.

Lippitt, V. 1966. Development of transportation in Communist China. *China Quarterly,* vol. 27, July. (Quoting Chang Kiangau 1943. *China's Struggle for Railroad Development.* New York: Day)

Liu, Alan P. L. 1975. *Communications and National Integration in Communist China.* Berkeley: University of California Press.

Liu Shao-chi. 1939. On the training of a Communist party member. In Conrad Brandt, Benjamin Schwartz, and John K. Fairbank, 1952, *A Documentary History of Chinese Communism, 1921–1950.* Cambridge: Harvard University Press.

Lu Hsun. 1977. *The True Story of Ah Q.* Trans. by Yang Hsien-yi and Gladys Yang. Beijing: Foreign Languages Press.

Lu Keng. 1979/80. The Chinese Communist press as I see it. *The Asian Messenger,* Winter/Spring.

McKeachie, Wilbert J., and Charlotte Lackner Doyle. 1966. *Psychology.* Reading, Mass.: Addison-Wesley.

Madsen, Richard. 1984. *Morality and Power in a Chinese Village.* Berkeley: University of California Press.

Mann, Jim. 1987. Protesters reshaping China political debate. *Los Angeles Times,* January 4.

Mao Tse-tung. 1954. *Selected Works of Mao Tse-tung.* New York: International Publishers.

———. 1965. On coalition government. *Selected works of Mao Tse-tung.* Peking: Foreign Languages Press.

Mathews, Jay, and Linda Mathews. 1983. *One Billion: A China Chronicle.* New York: Random House.

Moore, G. P. 1987. Chinese students' protests are far from academic. *Los Angeles Times,* January 5.

Morath, Inge, and Arthur Miller. 1979. *Chinese Encounters.* New York: Farrar, Straus, Giroux.

Morton, W. Scott. 1980. *China: Its History and Culture.* New York: Lippincott and Crowell.

Mosher, Steven W. 1983. *Broken Earth: The Rural Chinese.* New York: The Free Press/Macmillan.

Newsweek. 1984. China flexes its muscles on Hong Kong. December 17.

Pan Yunkang and Pan Naigu. 1983. Urban family structures and their changes. *Beijing Review,* February 28.

Pannell, Clifton W., and Laurence J. C. Ma. 1983. *China: The Geography of Development and Modernization.* London: V. H. Vinton and Sons and Edward Arnold.

Parish, William L., and Martin K. Whyte, eds. 1978. *Village and Family in Contemporary China.* Chicago: University of Chicago Press.

Rogers, Everett H., Xiaoyan Zhao, Zhongdang Pan, and Milton Chen. 1985. The Beijing audience study. *Communication Research,* vol. 12, no. 2.

Rudolph, Jorg-Meinhard. 1984. China's media: Fitting news to print. *Problems of Communism,* vol. 33, no. 4.

Schell, Orville. 1984. *To Get Rich Is Glorious: China in the Eighties.* New York: Pantheon Books.

Scherer, John L., ed. 1985. *China Facts and Figures Annual,* vol. 8. New York: Academic International Press.

Schlender, Brenton R. 1985. Shadowy Xinhua News Agency plays growing role in colony's life, politics. *Asian Wall Street Journal Weekly,* April 8.

Smith, Hedrick. 1976. *The Russians.* New York: Ballantine Books.

Tan Chen-lin. 1957. A preliminary study of the income and living standard of the peasants of China. *The People's Daily,* May 5.

Tong, Hollington K., ed. 1947. *The China Handbook, 1937–1943.* New York: Macmillan.

Tregear, T. R. 1980. *China: A Geographical Survey.* London: Hodder and Stoughton.

Wei Junyi. 1984. Women a new force in Chinese literature. *China Reconstructs,* October.

Weisskopf, Michael. 1983. China requires couples with two children to be sterilized in effort to slow growth. *Atlanta Journal-Constitution,* May 29.

Whyte, Martin King. 1977. Child socialization in the Soviet Union and China. *Studies in Comparative Communism,* vol. 10, no. 3.

Wong, David and Ian Chung. 1986. A break with old political taboos. *Hong Kong Standard,* September 1.

Wren, Christopher S. 1981. China turns love and chaos of 60's into a movie. *New York Times,* December 10.

_____. 1984. Music to mainland ears, off-key to Peking chiefs. *New York Times,* January 30.

Xiao Hongbin. 1984. Rural broadcasting network. *China Reconstructs,* March.

Yang, C. K. 1965. *Chinese Communist Society: The Family and the Village.* Cambridge: MIT Press.

Yang, Dori Jones. 1987. Guess what they watch in China on Sunday nights? *Business Week,* January 19.

Yu, Frederick T. C. 1964. *Mass Persuasion in Communist China.* New York: Praeger.

_____. 1979. China's mass communication in historical perspective. In Godwin C. Chu and Francis L. K. Hsu, *Moving a Mountain: Cultural Change in China.* Honolulu: University of Hawaii Press.

Zhou Zheng. 1981. Newspapers in China. *Beijing Review,* May 18.

Zhu Ling. 1984. China's feature films find way into world market. *China Daily,* August 21.

INDEX